Fired Up & F

**End Overwhelm. Turn Your Dreams
Into Inspired Action.**

Get Your Life Back – In 21 Days!

Fired Up & Focused

End Overwhelm. Turn Your Dreams Into Inspired Action. Get Your Life Back – In 21 Days!

By Racheal Cook

http://www.RachealCook.com

Copyright © 2015 Racheal Cook | The Yogipreneur LLC

The Yogipreneur LLC
9702 Gayton Road Suite #154
Richmond, VA 23238 United States

Don't miss the free 21 Day Fired Up & Focused Challenge that accompanies this book::

http://www.firedupandfocused.com

Ready to Get Your Life Back in 21 Days? Here's What You'll Learn::

Introduction

A few years ago, I was getting ready to kick off a weekend business retreat for 25 amazing women entrepreneurs. I asked everyone to introduce themselves to the group and share what they were hoping to get out of our weekend together.

"I'm so busy running my business, I don't know how to make time to create the programs and services that will help me grow."

"There's just so much to do and so many options... I don't even know where to start marketing and growing my business!"

"I left a job with just one boss - but now instead of being my own boss, I feel like I have a dozen bosses to answer to! How do I regain control of my biz and life?"

Then several of my private mentorship clients in attendance shared their biggest takeaways from our work together and it wasn't just the business and marketing strategy... it was the time we spent getting laser focused on what moved their biz forward *so they could have their life back.*

Once we put some very specific business practices in place – they no longer felt like they were spinning their wheels trying to figure out what to do next... they knew exactly what they should be focused on as the CEO of their business each and every day.

Are You Working ON Your Biz or IN Your Biz?

If you're a heart-centered entrepreneur... you started your business because you wanted to share your passion with the world!

You wanted to be the change!

And you wanted to make a life – not just a living – doing something meaningful.

But are you really doing what you love? Or are you finding yourself up to your eyeballs doing busy work?

Do you find yourself buried in to-dos like::

- Responding to a million emails {as soon as you clear your inbox, it just fills right back up!}

- Juggling your crazy schedule of classes, clients, and family obligations

- Getting clients appointments on the calendar {forget trying to just book in advance – you'd just love a consistent schedule!}

- Sending out and following up on invoices {because you need to get paid – like yesterday!}

- Planning for your next class or client session

- And the list goes on and on...

You know you need to work ON your biz, but who has the time when there is so much to do IN the day-to-day?

In 10 years of helping thousands of entrepreneurs, I've realized that too many of us find ourselves completely stressed out, overwhelmed, and on the verge of burnout because of one fatal mistake.

Spending too much time on the wrong tasks.

… Tasks that don't generate revenue …

… Tasks that don't attract new clients …

… Tasks that don't grow your biz !!!

And at the end of the day, these are tasks that eat up all your precious time! Time that could be much better spent serving more people or actually enjoying your life {the reason you actually started this business}!

Are You Running Your Business By Design {or Default}?

For so many entrepreneurs - myself included - one of the biggest reasons to start your own business is to be your own boss. Call all the shots. Make your own rules.

But the honest truth? Being your own boss is HARD.

Suddenly you're not only doing your client work - but you're also the marketing and sales team, customer service, and tech support. It's a lot more than most realize when they hang their shingle and declare they are open for business!

And that's where so many entrepreneurs get swept up in overwhelm.

No matter how amazing you are at what you DO for people, there is so much that goes into each and every client relationship. You're finding new clients. You're managing existing clients. You're doing whatever it is they pay you to do.

With so much to manage behind the scenes, it's no wonder that 80% of small businesses close their doors after a few short years. When you're business is running by default - reacting to every new situation that comes up - you'll always find yourself putting out fires.

Your Business is NOT an Emergency!

The difference between a business run by design and one run by default?

A business by design works FOR YOU {instead of you working your fingers to the bone to keep the doors open}.

A business by design is optimized to help you focus on the most important tasks that will move your business forward {instead of waking up and letting your inbox dictate your day}.

A business by design is what allows you, dear entrepreneur, an opportunity to experience the freedom, ease, and abundance you had hoped entrepreneurship would bring {and put an end to burnout, once and for all}.

When I hosted that business retreat a few years ago, it was such a huge light bulb moment for me! While I adore teaching business strategy and mindful marketing - I realized that all the strategy in the world wouldn't make a bit of difference if the women attending that retreat didn't have the space and systems in place to help them implement what they had learned.

That's why I created the <u>Fired Up & Focused Challenge – a free 21 Day Video Challenge</u> to help you work less and live more – and finally create the business and the life of your dreams.

It was a huge success! Not only did thousands of entrepreneurs join the challenge, but they started sending in email after email sharing amazing results::

- Filling their client docket
- Launching their first online program
- Confidently increasing their rates
- Doubling their monthly income
- Shaving over 10 hours off their work week

And these were just a few of the amazing results that Challengers have been seeing.

This book has taken everything from the Fired Up & Focused Challenge and condensed it into a step-by-step plan that you can use to simplify, streamline, and systematize your business.

Plus, if you're ready to take it to the next level, you can get the full Fired Up & Focused Challenge including short daily videos, exclusive book bonuses {including our CEO Planner}, and access to our private community of heart-centered entrepreneurs ready to cheer you on as you go for your dreams!

If you're ready to kiss burnout {and busywork} good-bye, you're gonna love getting Fired Up & Focused.

With Love + Gratitude,
Racheal Cook MBA

Get The Most From 21 Days
of Fired Up & Focused

I know you're chomping at the bit to kick off your 21 Days of Fired Up & Focused... but first, we've gotta talk about the most important lesson of this entire book.

Us entrepreneurs, we have no shortage of big ideas. Or new tips, tricks, and tactics to test out. There are shiny objects galore calling our name. But all that distraction is the number one reason that most entrepreneurs struggle to see real momentum in their business and life.

If you're ready to stop spinning your wheels and start seeing results, it's time to build the foundation of your success.

What is your foundation? It's a clear understanding of who you are and what matters most, to you. It's understanding why you are doing the work you're doing in the world. It's understanding who you are here to serve through your business. It's the vision that you have for your life, and business, for the years and months to come.

Too many entrepreneurs struggle because they never get clarity on the foundation of their business. Instead, they chase the next trend, shifting focus every six months, second-guessing every step they take.

There is so much noise about what it really takes to build a successful business. And these days, it seems like the hype is getting to a fever pitch! It's unreal how many are pimping the next magic bullet to breaking through to five-, six-, or seven-figure businesses.

We all start out thinking that modeling our business based on someone else's success is the answer. Everyone has a biz crush on the most successful entrepreneurs. But you've got to remember that what worked for them may not work for you. There are so many variables that make each of our businesses different, from::

- Our personalities
- Our strengths
- Our passions
- Our community
- Our experience
- Our goals
- Our desired lifestyle

Your business is NOT a piece of IKEA furniture! Even if you're offering the same type of services to the same audience for the same price tag as your biz crush - you won't see the same success unless you have a solid foundation.

Fired Up & Focused is here to help you build that solid foundation for success. Together, we're going to look at each area of your business and what you, dear CEO, should be investing your time and energy in {and where you need to stop wasting your precious time}. Once you have a foundation in place, you can tune out the hype and get down to business.

Over the next 21 days, we're gonna step-by-step plan, prioritize, and boost your productivity. Before we dive in, let's take 15 minutes to set yourself up for success!

1:: Make Time for Success

This sounds so simple, but the reason most entrepreneurs struggle to work ON the big picture of their business is they don't make time for it!

Look - you're an entrepreneur. There will always be work to be done. The to-do-list will never end. If you don't prioritize being the CEO of your business, you'll always feel like you're struggling to keep your head above water!

If you can give yourself 30 minutes a day for the next 21 days, you'll be amazed at how much you'll accomplish in just a few short weeks {and how much breathing room you'll finally have in your life}. **Schedule it now!**

2:: Try it On

Before you start flipping through this book and saying to yourself - *I already know about that... that won't work for me!* - I want you to commit to trying on each of these practices for just a few short weeks.

Look at Fired Up & Focused as a 21 Day experiment. Your job is to test out each of the daily challenges and see what works {and what doesn't} work for you and your business. As you get more clarity on your foundation, like a tailor you'll learn how to tweak and adjust these strategies to fit you and your business.

Resistance to change is the biggest reason why most people stay stuck. If you find yourself digging in your heels, crossing your arms, and saying "*But I don't wanna do it!*"… Then there is something going on below the surface.

Laying the foundation for your business is hard work! Entrepreneurship is truly the biggest personal development journey you could ever go on. You will be pushed outside of your comfort zone. You will face uncertainty. You will fight resistance. But once you're on the other side, you'll have a foundation that will help you design a business you love *that loves you back.*

3:: Find a Business BFF

People who make meaningful change in their habits, their lifestyle, and their business all have one thing in common - a support system. That's why I always recommend going through Fired Up & Focused with a Business BFF.

Entrepreneurship can be lonely. Most of our non-entrepreneur friends and family just don't get it! They don't understand what it feels like to have a burning desire to do and be more. They don't get that we'll take the big risks for the chance that we can live our dream.

A Business BFF is an accountability partner. A mastermind buddy. A fellow entrepreneur who is walking this path along side you. She's someone who understands the ups and downs of entrepreneurship, who is there to cheer you on when you feel like quitting, and who believes in your vision as much as you do.

If you don't have a Business BFF - make sure you join the Fired Up & Focused community to meet and mingle with other like-hearted entrepreneurs who are ready to cheer you on!

Let's Get Fired Up!

Day 1:: From Solopreneur to CEO

Right now, you may feel like you're struggling to juggle all the things that come along with this journey of entrepreneurship. If you've been feeling overwhelmed, you're not alone! You may have even had thoughts like these::

"I know I can do the work, but I don't know where to start."

"I want freedom, not to feel like a slave to my business."

"What do I really need to focus on?"

"I actually know what I need to do, okay, but I'm just scared shitless of failure."

"I'm completely overwhelmed with the day to day of my business; how am I supposed to find time to work on the big picture?"

These are exact words from people who reached out to me: heart-centered solopreneurs who were overwhelmed, stretched too thin, and on the verge of burnout.

It doesn't have to be this way! Business does not have to be so stressful.

Here's the thing - your greatest resource is the same 24-hours-in-a-day that everyone else has. The 168 hours a week.

In my work with thousands of heart-centered entrepreneurs, I've learned that the biggest difference between those who thrive and those who struggle to survive is all in how they approach this valuable resource. If you want to be a successful entrepreneur who's not only able to do work that you love, but have an amazing lifestyle to match, learning to maximize your time is the first step.

This is something that I get asked about all the time. I am a wife, I am a mother to three children under age 6, and, alongside my husband, I run two online businesses from our home, TheYogipreneur.com and RachealCook.com, that serve thousands of entrepreneurs around the world.

I've created this amazing, beautiful lifestyle where I can enjoy my family, my friends, make time for my self-care and health, and even pursue other hobbies and interests.

People ask how I manage to juggle so much or how I make it look so effortless. *The truth is that it's not effortless.* Every day, I make deliberate, conscious choices about where I'm going to invest my time and energy. This mindful approach to life and business has allowed me to design a lifestyle business I adore {with a lifestyle I have time to enjoy}!

The Successful CEO Framework

Since launching the Fired Up & Focused Challenge in 2014, I've taught this framework to thousands of heart-centered entrepreneurs. If you've ever wondered about the difference between working IN your business and working ON your business, this model will help you see where you'll get the best return on your time and energy investment into your biz.

5 Core Tasks for Entrepreneurs

Marketing · Business Development + Education · Work with Clients · Customer Service · Admin/Ops

1:: Administrative and Operations

Administrative and operations are the nitty-gritty, day-to-day tasks that happen behind closed doors in every business. These internal tasks must happen to keep your business running smoothly, but this is where I see a lot of entrepreneurs spending too much of their valuable time. These are tasks like::

- Organizing paperwork and receipts
- Sending, paying, and tracking invoices
- Updating bookkeeping and filing taxes
- Updating your customer database
- Research for upcoming projects

While admin/ops is all honestly important work that is essential for keeping the business running like a well-oiled machine, it always takes more time than you'd think.

And as the CEO of your biz, it's essential to recognize that these tasks are not revenue generating.

Starting today and throughout Fired Up & Focused, you'll learn ways to streamline and systematize these admin/ops areas of your business so that you can shift your attention to the revenue generating activities that allow you to better serve your business and your clients.

2:: Customer Service

Customer service can feel a little tricky because while it's not directly revenue generating, it can make all the difference in how your customers feel about you and your business {which in turn affects how many of said customers turn into raving fans who regularly send referrals your way}.

Taking the time to design a seamless customer experience will not only free up your time, but will help your clients feel well taken care of. What tasks fall under customer service?

- Scheduling client sessions
- Managing and responding to emails
- Managing and responding to voicemails
- Sending out appointment reminders
- Sending out appointment follow-up
- Mailing customer appreciation cards and gifts

With a little thoughtfulness and planning, you'll be able to make it easy for your clients to work with you {and completely WOW them with the personal touches}. It pays off big time to systematize customer service so you can pass these tasks off to an assistant, and get back to being a CEO!

3:: Working with Clients

The next core task area is where the value exchange actually happens - your clients have paid for your time, expertise, or the product you've created.

For many solopreneurs, this means that you're getting paid dollars for hours to do work that you love. You may be working one-on-one with clients or one-to-many by serving groups of people at a time.

Or you may have a passive business model where you don't actually have to be there in order to help people, but serve them through an online course or info product.

Whatever your current business model, this is your value exchange. You're offering something of value to people in order to solve a problem or fulfill a desire.

As the CEO, you've got to optimize your business model for two things::

1. **Profitability**:: Earning more revenue than your business expenses so that you can pay yourself a comfortable {live-able} income.
2. **Sustainability**:: Ensuring that your return on investment {ROI} for your time and energy is

maximized so you can actually enjoy the lifestyle you're creating!

It's easy to think about optimizing your business model for profits, but you can't forget to optimize for sustainability. This is really key. I see a lot of clients who've nearly burnt themselves out because they've become a bottleneck in their business.

When it comes to growing your business, you really only have a few choices::

Option 1 - Add more clients.

Option 2 - Increase your prices.

Option 3 - Add more leveraged or passive income streams.

When entrepreneurs focus on adding more clients, once their calendar is full they can't grow their business anymore because they've simply run out of time. They try to make more space in the calendar, and end up sacrificing their own family time, personal time, and self-care. They lose sleep, family time, and their lifestyle.

When your calendar is maxed out, the next option is to increase your prices. This is a great strategy, but unless you're delivering dramatically MORE value, you'll again create a ceiling for your income.

The best option to maximize for profitability and sustainability is often to look for ways to begin offering multiple programs, products, and services that diversify your income streams. As you begin to build income streams that are less dependent on trading dollars for hours, you'll create more ease and freedom in your business.

4:: Business Development and Education

So many solo entrepreneurs either avoid business development all together or use it as the ultimate procrastination strategy, going down rabbit hole after rabbit hole of edu-tainment, without actually implementing anything.

I get it. There is so much to learn! There are so many options. There are so many different programs and services and things you can add to your business. It can get overwhelming. And when we get so overwhelmed, our instinct is just to say, "Oh, I'll get to that someday."

Well, my friend, "someday" is not a day of the week. You've gotta start building business development and education time into your calendar so that you can begin to see some real momentum and real growth in your business.

5:: Marketing + Making Money

Your marketing can have the most dramatic long-term and short-term impact on the profitability and sustainability of your business. If done right, this can have the biggest return on investment of your time, energy, and money for each hour that you spend working on it. Period.

Now that you can see the five core areas you need to focus on as a solopreneur, we're going to dive deeper throughout the Fired Up and Focused series into each area to help you find the right mix of time and energy you should be investing into each area. This will help you move away from being the worker bee 24/7 so you can begin focusing your most precious resource - your time - into CEO level tasks to create more profitability and sustainability in your business.

80/20:: The Secret to Working Less and Living More

Called the Pareto Principle, the 80/20 rule was developed by an Italian economist in the 1700s. Pareto discovered that 20% of the inputs yielded 80% of the outputs. He started looking across all sorts of different industries - from agriculture to manufacturing to just about anything - and discovered that the 80/20 rule applied across the board.

What does that mean for you? It means 20% of the tasks you're focused on in your business yield 80% of the results {and 80% of the tasks you're doing are only contributing to 20% of your results}.

Our goal is to start understanding what those 20% tasks should be.

What are those things that really move us forward?

How can we spend more of our time there so that we can get the maximum results with the most efficient {i.e. least} amount of effort?

Our goal is to focus your time and energy on results-based activities; to say *no* to busy work and to say *yes* to results.

Being productive for the sake of crossing more off your to-do list doesn't always yield real results in your business. Once you understand which tasks will dramatically move your business forward, you'll be able to cross off many of the tasks that currently eat up all your valuable time. Understanding and implementing the 80/20 rule into my business is why I've been able to double my business each year while really only working about 25 hours a week.

It all begins by understanding how you're spending your time.

Most entrepreneurs are spending their time backwards. They've basically created jobs for themselves where they're dealing with busy work all the time. Too many solopreneurs mismanage their time within the Successful Solopreneur Framework.

One of my favorite assignments for my clients is to have them track their working hours. When they report back, we often realize that the biggest reason why their business isn't growing is because they spent all their time on customer service, administrative, and operations level tasks and they wind up with too little time - if any - for business development or marketing.

If that's you and you're frustrated that your business just isn't gaining the momentum you'd like, we've gotta flip that whole model on its head. You should be able to open up your calendar every single week ready to spend your time on the 20% of tasks that yield 80% of results.

How Successful CEOs Spend Time

Marketing

Business Dev + Ed

Working with Clients

Customer Service

Admin/Ops

What are the 20% tasks that you should spend time on every week? Marketing and business development.

As we start shifting towards this model, you'll notice we're minimizing customer service tasks; we're minimizing administrative tasks; we're minimizing operations tasks. It does not mean that they disappear. These are things that all businesses have to take care of, but these are things that you can streamline, systematize, and when you're ready, outsource to an assistant or team member.

You must be focused on the big picture. *You* must be the heart and soul of your business. **You must do the work of a CEO.**

Day 1:: Fired Up & Focused Challenge!

Time for inspired action. Here's your challenge to begin to optimize your business to the 80/20 rule and step into your role as CEO of your business::

1:: Where are you spending your time in your business?

Does your time look like the first graph? The pyramid where most of your time is spent being a busy worker bee: you're dealing with customer service, administration, operations, you feel like you're always busy, but you're not really getting anywhere?

Or are you a successful CEO? Are you spending most of your time looking at CEO-level work: the big picture, the marketing, the business development, and the education?

Or, are you somewhere in between? It's a spectrum. We're not all one or the other and it does change from time to time.

But, it's really clear that you have to be honest with yourself with where you are right now so that we can have a baseline and start moving you from busy worker bee to successful CEO.

2:: How much time can you commit to CEO tasks each week?

Play this smart; look at how much time you can realistically commit to and stick to right now in your business. *If it's just 30 minutes a day, that's totally fine!*

Stick to it, commit to it, and you'll already be on a better path because you're mindfully focusing your time to those high-level tasks in your business.

If you're able to give yourself a little bit more, that's great too. Don't overextend yourself - set yourself up for success. It's easier to add time little by little than to try to throw yourself into the deep end, struggle, then give up because you overcommitted.

3:: Block out CEO time in your calendar every day.

Make an appointment for successful, high-level, CEO time every single day and soon you will see that higher value input delivers higher value output in your business.

Day 2:: Are you Mind-FULL or Mindful?

Modern society has most of us struggling to focus our attention on one thing at a time. It's just not easy for a lot of people these days, if it ever was. The average attention span has now fallen to just 8 seconds!

We're mentally loaded with all of the things that we have to do... and then our senses are bombarded with social media pings, inbox notifications, distractions and interruptions.

When your mind is this cluttered, *you are never going to do your best work*. You're going to feel overwhelmed and completely burned out just by the pace of your life, not to mention keeping up with all the must-dos in your business.

If you find your head spinning about all the things you have to do, want to do, should do, could do… your focus is going to be lost on all of them; you'll never be 100% present.

You'll become anxious and either burnout or procrastinate in your efforts.

Move from Mind-Full to Mindful

Let's free up some bandwidth.

Every once in a while I need to create some mental white space, to get all of those thoughts about things to be done out of my brain and on to paper.

Sure, you've probably done this before. It's a to-do list right? Yes and no.

I call this a Brain Dump, and here are the rules:

- Grab a piece of paper and a pen.
- Set a timer for 15 minutes.
- Write down everything in your mental to-do list.
- Do not censor or edit!
- Include both personal and business-related thoughts.
- Include the urgent gotta get done right now tasks and the months away tasks.
- When the timer goes off and you're done, set it for 5 minutes and keep going!

The no censoring, no editing rules are key; this is most likely going to be your biggest To-Do list ever! Do not panic! Once you've cleared out the to-do list from your brain, resist the urge to do all the things.

First, we're going to prioritize.

This is really essential {and fun!} because you'll likely discover that a good number of the tasks that have been sucking away your mental energy really aren't things you need to devote much time or energy on!

Prioritization is key for managing this big master to do list. But still, one giant ordered list isn't a very good guide for managing your time and tasks. You need to know what needs to be done right now, what can be handled later, what you need to make time for, and what you can outsource to someone else's to-do list.

I follow a strategy from the book *7 Habits of Highly Effective People* by Stephen Covey. He advises splitting up your to-do list into four simple categories by importance and urgency.

Habits of Highly Effective People

Quadrant 1:: Urgent and Important {aka 911 Tasks}

The first quadrant is for urgent and important tasks. So these are the near-emergencies; they have to get done right now. If they don't, something bad will happen.

Now if you're finding yourself with a lot of tasks in this area, you're probably stressed out, anxious, and maybe even fearful. This is not the way to run a conscious business. Your business is not an emergency, and feeling like you're constantly putting out fires is not how we get you to the life and business you're really dreaming of.

You must ultimately minimize what falls in this area of your to do list, and manage your time and tasks so it stays near-empty forever.

Quadrant 2:: Urgent but Not-Important {aka Assistant Tasks}

The next quadrant is not as important but still urgent. These are the tasks that have to get done all the time, but they're not going to make or break your business.

One example could be the tasks you have to complete once you get a new client: sending a welcome packet, sending out an agreement and invoice, setting up scheduling, etc. These are tasks that must be done but you should be able to streamline and systematize.

Urgent means it needs to get done when it comes up. Usually these are things you can prepare for in advance so you aren't constantly re-creating the wheel each time. These systems will ensure that you can complete these tasks quickly, that nothing falls through the cracks, and make it easier to pass off to an assistant.

Quadrant 3:: Not-Urgent + Not-Important {aka Stop Doing Tasks}

The next quadrant is for the less important and less urgent tasks. Hopefully, as you read that you realized that...these are tasks that you don't really need to be doing at all.

I see a lot of people filling up their day with tasks that are ultimately not important and don't drive their business forward.

Here you need to start questioning: if it's not important to your business, if it's not driving your business forward or helping you achieve a goal, and if it's not urgent, then why are you doing it? Can you stop doing it? Can you just cut it out altogether and see what happens?

I often get asked what kinds of tasks fall under this area - and honestly it depends. That's why you must question every item on your to-do list. If it's not actually driving a result, cross it off!

Quadrant 4:: Important but Not Urgent {aka the CEO Sweet Spot}

The final quadrant is for important but less urgent tasks. These things will move your business forward, but generally these tasks require more focused time for you to do your best work.

Remember talking about the 20% tasks in Day 1? These are CEO level tasks:: marketing, business development, investing in your own business education, and your own coaching, leadership, or personal development work.

As the CEO of your business, your goal is to spend the majority of your time here.

Everything else either needs to be handled quickly, systematized, streamlined, or discarded so you can set your sights and mental energy on things that deliver wealth, freedom, and value back to you and your business.

Day 2:: Fired Up & Focused Challenge!

Time to get into inspired action, and go from having a mind full of to-do's to a mindful plan for success.

1:: Spend 15 Minutes on a Brain Dump.

- Grab a piece of paper and a pen.
- Set a timer for 15 minutes.
- Write down everything in your mental to-do list.
- Do not censor or edit!
- Include both personal and business-related thoughts.
- Include the urgent gotta get done right now tasks and the months away tasks.
- When the timer goes off and you're done, set it for 5 minutes and keep going!

You've emptied your mind. Now to prioritize mindfully! I recommend splitting the business from the personal this time, since we'll be looking for opportunities to cut down on your list in the future.

2:: Prioritize Your To-Do List

Download the handouts and worksheets at http://www.firedupandfocused.com/book.

If you don't have the worksheet, you can grab another page and draw out your four quadrants.

Go through your brain-dump from above and transfer the tasks that need to get done in the next 90 days into your prioritization matrix. Tasks that are beyond the next 90 days can be kept in an Idea Parking Lot {nothing fancy - just a document where you keep your running list of ideas}.

Once you have your to-do list sorted into the right quadrants, prioritize them. Then you'll have the confidence to know exactly what needs your attention first and that you're focusing on the right tasks at the right time.

3:: Start Working Your To-Do List

First - Do the Urgent + Important Tasks. You may want to make note of any tasks here that are repeating, so that you can plan better next time around, create a system, and prevent them from becoming urgent emergencies.

Second - Do the Urgent but Not Important Tasks. These need your attention because there's something absolutely crucial you must do as you check these tasks off your list. While you work on these tasks, make a checklist as you go so it will be easier to pass off or complete faster next time.

Next - Schedule Time for Important but Not Urgent Tasks. Schedule time in your calendar to make it happen. It's that simple. These 20% CEO level tasks are likely the ones that will grow your business the most, and are things that only you can do. Invest in successful CEO time on your calendar, invest in the big picture, the ideas, marketing plans, business development, and education.

Finally - Cross Off Any Not Important or Urgent Tasks.
For today, take a long hard look at the Not Urgent + Not Important list. Stop doing it, stop wasting your time, stop wasting up mental energy. Just focus on the things that are ultimately important in your business.

Day 3:: End Procrastination and Get Things Done!

There is something you've got to get done; something important that you know is going to drive your business forward.

But you're kind of dreading it, so you put it off. ***You procrastinate.***

Why do we procrastinate? Everybody does this. Every single one of us has procrastinated something important at some point of time... even though we know it's holding us back from the success we truly desire. So why do we do this to ourselves?

Maybe you just hate the task. In that case, we can take a look and see if it's something you even need to do at all. Systematize it, streamline it, or pass it off to someone else.

The other thing that could be happening is that you might just be worried about how big a task is and that makes you feel like it's going to take forever.

This happens all the time when there is a big project that you want to do, and you know it's going to drive your business forward, but you also know it's a pretty big undertaking. It could be creating a new offering. It could be writing an eBook. It could be putting together something that you know ultimately has a lot of steps.

If you're still struggling with super urgent tasks and setting up systems for your business, you may tell yourself, "I don't have time for the big project; there's just too much to do in my day to day."

Or you tell yourself you'll make time for it on the weekend... and then realize you're working on your business seven days a week.

This is not what successful CEOs do. They know that their evenings and their weekends really need to be used to step away, to relax, to rejuvenate, to reap the rewards of their hard work.

Not to mention - if you're like me and have ever tried to focus on good work on a weekend when your family is wanting time with you, you've probably realized that it's impossible to give both your family and your business 100%.

It's crucial that we learn how to focus during our regular work hours.

As an entrepreneur, it's often freeing to think about how we're not locked into a 9-to-5... but if you fail to make your work time sacred and keep the distractions away, you'll find yourself working or thinking about work during your off hours too.

"We didn't leave a 9-to-5 to work 24/7!"
- Nikki Elledge Brown

Master the Art of Productive Procrastination

I'm going to share with you a strategy that I use called Productive Procrastination. It sounds completely counterintuitive but this is one of the strategies that has allowed me to produce so much content on a regular basis for not just one, but two, online businesses.

And, ultimately, it's allowed me to work less than 25 hours a week on my business so that I can enjoy my afternoons, my evenings, and my weekends with my family.

It all starts with a simple timer.

This technique is actually called the Pomodoro Technique. It was developed by an Italian grad student who realized he was struggling to study really big and important pieces of information.

So he grabbed a kitchen timer. It happened to be shaped like a tomato - in Italian tomato is pomodoro. He set the timer for 25 minutes, and sat down and studied.

The timer went off and he gave himself a little bit of a break; walked around, did something relaxing for five minutes. And then he came back, set the timer again and just got right back in the zone.

It is amazing! He realized that he could train himself to get really super focused using this technique. As a result he was able to do what he previously thought he could only do during long stretches of time in very short focused bursts.

The technique allows you to hack your brain. It's going to retrain the way that you focus on things. These short bursts of focused energy are great since our brain doesn't naturally like to slog through long periods of high-level thinking.

Our brain loves these short, focused bursts of energy with purpose, drive, and focus. No distraction. No end-all-be-all goal.

In 25 minutes you're not going to write an entire eBook. You're not going to create your entire new offering. But you will get into the zone and build momentum very, very quickly.

This technique is all about making incremental progress instead of just putting things off or forcing yourself to slog through like six straight hours of work. It's something that will allow you to get the important things done with more focus in less time.

Day 3:: Fired Up & Focused Challenge!

1:: Choose 3 tasks off your To-Do List for today.

Are they things that you're certain can be completed start-to-finish during your work hours today? If so, excellent, you already know you can do everything that absolutely needs to get done, and using the Pomodoro technique to do it will help you see how much more quickly you can complete these tasks.

If your urgent + important list includes more open ended, ongoing projects, then you'll want to set benchmarks for them to better measure your progress. Setting and reaching benchmarks will measure your accomplishments toward the project, keeping you motivated, and preventing that vague, immeasurable feeling of "I worked on it some more."

2:: Set your timer for 25 minutes.

Take your list, get a timer {use a kitchen timer, your phone, or the clock timer on your computer. I prefer a manual kitchen timer because the tactile object helps make time more real and tangible than if I used just a digital tool}, and start working on your list in 25-minute intervals.

3:: Take a 5 minute break.

During your 5 minute breaks, really cut off from work. Stand up. Walk around. Grab a healthy snack. Go outside breathe some fresh air. Have a personal dance party. Write a thank you card. Go give your nanny a bathroom break and your kiddo some snuggles. Call your mom.

4:: Then clock yourself back in for another solid 25 minutes.

Fully free again from distraction and all the items on your list.

Do one thing. Do it for 25 minutes.

5:: Rinse and Repeat.

I generally set up my Pomodoros in a 90 minute cycle:: 25 - 5 - 25 - 5 - 25. Then give myself a good 30 minute break. You can structure these based on your own natural rhythms - some like to do 45 - 15 - 45 - 15.

Done deliberately and repeatedly, you'll train your brain to stop trying to escape into some distracting thought or action during your work time, because you'll know you already set aside little breaks intermittently during your day.

You can get 100% focused work in those 25 min, and 100% of relaxation in those 5 min. And I promise you, you'll be amazed how much more productive your time will become!

Day 4:: Creating a Sacred Workspace

I hear from people over and over again about their really crazy schedules. I know for a lot of solopreneurs working from home {often while juggling a family or other responsibilities} that your daily schedule can look kind of disjointed.

Feeling like you're running around makes it pretty hard to create the sacred space that you need in order to do your highest, best level work.

I'm going to share with you a technique that will allow you to quickly create that sacred space wherever you are so that you can do your highest, best level work every time you sit down.

But first, I want to talk about yoga.

There is something magical that happens when you go into a studio for your yoga practice. The moment you step through the studio doors, your body starts to have a physiological response.

Your breath starts to deepen, your shoulders start to fall back and down. Your chest expands, and your entire body feels like it's taking a big sigh and becomes grounded again. It's really quite amazing what happens when you go through something as simple as stepping through a doorway.

But the truth is...the magic that happens in the studio does not need a studio for it to happen.

Rituals Create a Sacred Space

Often people think that it's the studio walls themselves that create the atmosphere, the aura for that sense of grounding, of centering. That's not true.

It's the ritual.

It's the things that you're doing leading up to the practice and wrapping up the practice that create this sacred atmosphere wherein we practice yoga.

Let's look at the practice of yoga through this lens. There are three stages that you go through. Three different parts of this full cycle.

First is the opening stage. For most, we start with a round of ohm, and may have a guided meditation or a sun salutation before beginning the core practice itself.

The yoga movements are actually the second piece of the yoga class; the opening rituals have prepared you mentally and physically for it, and you sink in fully focused.

When the practice ends, we have another ritual before stepping out into our lives: a savasana, guided meditation, or chant of ohm.

There's always something clearly defining the start or end of a yoga practice: this is why so many people experience that something amazing happened during that time.

Once you start a ritual, your mind chatter starts to quiet. And once you have a specific ritual that you do in connection to another activity, your brain will pair the two, and the experience together will become greater than the sum of its parts: it's a Pavlovian response.

In the case of your yoga class, you're training your brain to quiet down and to calm down so that you can be engaged and present for the practice. You stop asking yourself why or what's next. You just start the ritual and then you can very easily stay present and do the next thing that you have to do without a whole lot of thought, without a whole lot of struggle over what to do.

This is what's really important, when the ritual ends, when you go through the process of wrapping it up, wrapping up your practice, you feel complete. You feel like you can transition and move on. This is something that I think a lot of people are missing once they leave the yoga studio and go back to the real world.

I began to study the power of rituals while reading *The Creative Habit* by Twyla Tharp. This is one of my favorite books of all time and I highly, highly recommend it.

Tharp is a famous choreographer and dancer who has produced an incredible body of work. Through this book *The Creative Habit*, she talks about the power of rituals and just plain getting started.

For her the ritual that kicks off her day is waking up at 5:30 in the morning, getting into a cab, and going to the gym for a two-hour workout.

It's not the two-hour workout that starts her day. It's getting into the cab.

She has realized that once she gets into the cab, she's on her way. She doesn't even have to question it any longer. She's on a path of predictable actions that will her get her where she ultimately wants to go.

Once I started looking at how creative people like Twyla - or Steven Pressfield who wrote *The War of Art* - approach work, I realized that many creative people seem to be doing something that the rest of us don't know about.

They have these little, tiny, seemingly meaningless rituals that they do every single day without fail that help them get into a creative mental state very, very quickly without hemming or hawing or procrastinating or struggling with themselves about it.

We can do the same thing with our work.

Again, just like our yoga practice, there are three key stages of this: there is a preparation; there is the work itself; and then there is the closing of our work time.

Once you figure out a ritual to prepare you for your work and a ritual to close your work, you'll have created this sacred space in between where you'll be more highly engaged, distraction-free, soulful, and present.

This is powerful! This will allow you to do your best work without having to endure a long build up to it, or punish yourself for not being on top of things all the time.

How I Start and Finish Each Workday

I want to share with you my own little rituals and help you break these down in the hopes that more examples may help you find the idea for a perfect ritual of your own::

My workday begins once I've taken my kids to preschool. I drive back and brew a fresh pot of coffee, and let Mitchell, my youngest, skip off to play with our nanny.

I close the doors to my office, I light a candle, I put on my headset and cue up some relaxing music, and I open my to-do list.

This instantly helps me to get laser focused. I sit down knowing exactly what I need to start working on. It's not even a question.

I don't have to shuffle anything. I don't have to check my email. I know exactly what I need to do to start my work.

My closing ritual is basically the same, but in reverse:: I write out my must-do-tomorrow list, I take off my headphones, I blow out the candle, I open the doors from my office which lead into our family room.

I confidently end work-Racheal's day, and step out as mama-Racheal, sweeping up the baby from the nanny and covering him in kisses.

The Must-Do Tomorrow List

The key piece for my closing ritual is my must-do-tomorrow list. This is something that I've been doing for about the last six or so years. I learned the habit during my more traditional business consulting role for a Fortune 500 company.

I realized that people who were getting things done were the people who sat down and knew exactly what they needed to do that morning. They didn't have to shuffle anything; they didn't have to question anything.

They knew exactly what they needed to do.

The concept comes from a story about the 1900s steel tycoon Charles Schwab. Schwab had a consultant named Ivy Lee who offered to increase the productivity of Schwab's people, and let Schwab decide what the results were worth. Schwab said sure, go ahead.

Lee taught each executive to sit down at the end of each day and create a list. The list contains only the six most important tasks to be completed the next day.

Each morning they should start the day by working on the first item on that list and not move on until it was completed. After a few months of this, Schwab sent a check to Lee for $25,000. Today, it would be nearly half a million dollars!

This simple, simple practice is ties up any mental loose ends that I might have. My workday is done, whatever work must come next will come when tomorrow's begins.

The amazing part is that this end-of-day ritual allows me to start my mornings off great! I never sit down to work in a fog; I never have to prioritize during my mornings. I already have the plan.

Now, limiting the number of tasks to 6 {or fewer!} is really important. Personally, I limit mine to a maximum of three.

I try not to overload myself with too many things to do, and I've practiced enough prioritization, planning, and delegation that::

1) I don't have urgent little tasks pressing on me as my team manages the majority of my admin/ops and customer service tasks
2) I am working on the big-picture, creative tasks of a CEO that demand dedicated time and focus

I find that my best work comes when I'm focusing more deeply on only 1 or 2 tasks... 3 if I'm really, really feeling productive. If I can get even just one big CEO-sized thing done each day then I know I've set myself up for success.

Day 4:: Fired Up & Focused Challenge!

Time to get into inspired action! Let's create your Must Do Tomorrow list. Now this is a simple and quick little practice, but there are some key points to making it work best for you::

1) Important Tasks Only. First, we must understand the type of tasks that belong on this list. At the end of each day you write down the most important tasks to do tomorrow. These aren't the most urgent tasks. These are the most important tasks - huge differentiator here. Focus on the important, not urgent, is how we live into our role as the CEO.

2) Make Tasks Check-Off-Able. The other key here is that the 6 items on your list be check-off-able tasks, not projects. A project is made up of lots of numerous steps that are completed in sequence, some of which may be delegated, etc. If working on a bigger project, pulling out the bite size tasks will help you make more progress.

This is how you set yourself up for success. Breaking things down helps make sure you feel you've accomplished something at the end of the day.

The next morning, start with the first task and focus on that task until it's completed.

Now this is where those pomodoros come in really handy! You start with task number 1 as your first pomodoro for 25 minutes. Take a break. If that task isn't completed, you sit down and finish it in the next round. And if it's not finished then, it goes in your next day's must-do-tomorrow list.

By creating this sacred space of your workday, and having it closed off on both ends, you can be fully devoted to your work, free of distraction, and you'll start to really guarantee that you get 100% focus and maximum efficiency from yourself.

Day 5:: Ready for Less Working & More Living?

By now you should have made some great progress in prioritizing and planning your tasks in your business... which means measuring the time you're spending in your business becomes a whole new game.

As a mamapreneur, work/life balance is something that I get asked about ALL. THE. TIME. Yes, I'm a CEO. Yes, I'm running a rapidly growing business. But ya' know what? My family, my health, and my downtime aren't just a luxury - _they are a priority_ if I'm going to continue doing what I do!

I have people asking me constantly, "_How is it that you seem to get everything done? I'm so busy... I can't find time to have family dinner or take a weekend off or get my booty to a yoga class!_"

I hear you. It's not easy to make big changes in how you approach your life and business! But today, I'll shed some light on how you can begin to manage it all with a little more ease, a little more grace, and find more white space in your week.

The goal is not to pack every single minute of your day and your week with a scheduled to-do. It's to give yourself a flexible framework so that you can experience more ease and more flow throughout your week.

Juggling the 5 Balls of Life

I love this story that I heard for the first time when I was in college. It comes from the 1996 Georgia Tech Commencement Speech by Bryan Dyson who was the CEO at Coca-Cola at the time.

"Imagine life as a game in which you're juggling five balls in the air. You name them work, family, health, friends and spirit. You must keep all the balls in the air. But, you soon understand that work is a rubber ball. If you drop it, it will bounce back. The other four balls--family, health, spirit, and friends--they're made of glass. If you drop one of them, they will be irrevocably scuffed, marked, nicked, damaged or even shattered. They will never be the same. You must understand that and strive for balance in your life."

It's up to US to make space for what matters. I've really taken this to heart because I come from a family of extremely hardworking entrepreneurs. I remember so many times growing up when I would watch my dad burn himself out over and over again just trying to make payroll for his employees. I remember that him coming home from a 10-12 hour day exhausted and with no energy for anything other than zoning out in front of the TV.

It really hit me hard when I began to meet the same type of burnout in my traditional corporate consulting career. When anxiety attacks struck, I realized that if I didn't make it a priority to take care of myself, my health, my well-being, my relationships, my spirit, I risked winding up in a place where all those areas of my life would not be there for me. I knew things had to change.

I made a plan to create more white space around my workweek to help ensure that those five core areas of your life get the attention they deserve.

Make Space for What Matters Most

I call this system a Model Calendar. It's nothing super fancy and it's not even something that's a precise, structured tool. This isn't where you're going to map out every single minute of your day for an entire week. Personally, I need a balance between structure and flexibility.

If you make your schedule too concrete, and a traffic jam, late lunch, or phone call can throw it off and make you feel like your day is ruined, or worse, that you've failed.

If you happen to be someone who's got a family, you've got a spouse, you've got friends, you've got all these different things going on, you'll be really glad when a kid gets sick or someone needs your help and you have the flexibility that allows you to take care of them.

At the same time, I need a system in place to make sure that I'm getting the five core task areas of my business accomplished every single week. I find that if I don't make the time in the plans, it's really easy to skip by them one week, then suddenly weeks go by and oops, I forgot to write my blog post this month.

Start By Prioritizing Your Family + Personal Time First.

I know this sounds counter-intuitive to a lot of business-minded people, but those are the same people who will work forever and find themselves out of time for family and self-care.

As entrepreneurs, we tend to put work first above all else. We don't make quality time with our families. We don't get ourselves to the gym. But you must put yourself and your family first, so commit to essential non-work time by scheduling it.

That includes your personal time. I'm an introvert; I need lots of personal time. I need lots of down time. If I don't have a book in my hand for at least an hour a day, I am not a happy camper. I make sure that I schedule time for myself into my calendar, right after time with family.

By taking care of myself and my family first, I avoid burnout in my work.

Create Boundaries Between Work Time + Personal Time.

Only after you've made time for life should you mark in your office hours. Now, I think this is really crucial. I find a lot of entrepreneurs are just working whenever there's time to work. As a result, they're working 24/7/365. They don't have any boundaries between their work time and their personal time. They haven't put the rituals in place to separate their sacred workspace from their life.

Now, I understand that not everybody has a consistent schedule. Remember, this is something to move towards, and I've found that it just helps to have dedicated office hours when you are working on your business.

This happens automatically for me because my office hours are when my children are in school. It makes a huge difference for me because I can be 100% present for my business when it's time to work, and I can be 100% present for my family when we're together.

Schedule a Regular CEO Date.

The next important things to schedule are CEO dates. I'll tell you much more about the CEO date in just a few pages. For right now, you just need to know that it's a crucial element to focusing on the big picture of your business.

I found if you don't make it happen, if you don't put these CEO dates in your calendar, then you tend to fall back into worker-bee mode and start to stray from the CEO-level mindset and work where you should live in your business. Start with one hourly CEO date each week.

Block Out Time for Your Successful Solopreneur Tasks.

Now it's time to put in the five core task areas. I schedule these in blocks because the individual tasks you're doing will probably change. Maybe one week you're writing blog posts, and another week you're connecting with people from a networking event. Those individual tasks will change.

The goal here is to make sure that you're touching on each of these core task areas at least once a week so that nothing gets left behind and you continue to make forward motion.

As you start to do that, you'll also want to begin to group like with like. Often you'll find tasks that you're doing over and over again in your business, and you'll get into a flow if you have them all grouped together.

For example, if you are working with clients, I find that it's much easier to get into a groove when I'm on the phone with my clients if they're scheduled back to back instead of having one client here, one client there and another tomorrow. Grouping like with like can help you get into the zone and be really engaged with what you're doing that day.

Along those same lines, batching recurring tasks is incredibly powerful. By this, I mean things that you have to do on a regular basis. They might fall under admin/ops, they might fall under marketing. These are things that you have committed to doing on a regular basis in your business.

Some of the best tasks to batch might be creating new outgoing content for your newsletter or your blogs, preparing for clients sessions or workshops that you're teaching, or just knocking out all those admin/ops tasks.

A Peek into My Week

Now that I've given you a really high level overview, I want to walk you through how I actually structure my week. Before I show you this, I want to let you know a couple of things.

One:: This can be adapted to just about anybody and any business. I promise. You do not have to do exactly what I'm doing. It's all about making it work for you, for your schedule and, honestly, for your family and any other priorities in your life.

Two:: This will change. It changes a lot, especially if you have young children or something else that naturally causes a lot of variation from week to week. I make it a priority to check back in every 3 months to make sure that I'm really sticking to my calendar and that it's really working for me. If it's not, if I find myself neglecting an area of my life or business, then I know that it's time to go in and tweak it.

With that being said, I'm going to show you exactly how I set up my model calendar each and every week.

I always start with my family and my self-care time. If I don't plug it in, I will get out of bed and check my email first thing. I will work straight through the lunch hour. I will not allow myself an evening off. I will find a reason to work because the truth is, I love it. I love doing what I do.

Writing family and self-care time into my calendar ensures that I'm taking care of myself, that I'm present with my family and that I'm making space, especially for me for my own self-care and my own down time.

Model Calendar

	Mon	Tues	Wed	Thurs	Fri
8			Family/Self-Care		
9					
10					
11					
12			Self Care		
1					
2					
3					Family/Relax
4					
5	Family Night	Date Night	Ballet	Game Night	Movie Night

The Fired Up & Focused Challenge
Day 5

The next block of time I account for is office hours. You can see if fits so cleanly in here. The perfectionist side of me is very happy with how neat it looks here.

It did not always used to be this way.

It was more complicated when my husband was working full time as a teacher. But, now that he's home with me working on our business, both of our calendars have opened up and fit with each other. Just know that this time could shift for you and it's okay.

Model Calendar

	Mon	Tues	Wed	Thurs	Fri
8			Family/Self-Care		
9					
10			Office Hours		
11					
12			Self Care		
1					
2			Office Hours		Family/Relax
3					
4					
5	Family Night	Date Night	Ballet	Game Night	Movie Night

The Fired Up & Focused Challenge
Day 5

Once you have your office hours set, schedule your weekly CEO date next. I love my CEO date; it's a great way to start and wrap up my week.

My CEO date is when I'm checking everything that's going on in my business against my one year plan, my quarterly plan, my monthly plan. Then I can decide on the highest priority tasks I need to focus on for that week.

I start my week knowing exactly what needs to happen for the days ahead, and I wrap my week the same way. Again, it's a ritual, and it's similar to the must-do-tomorrow list, but focused on breaking down those big picture projects into more check-off-able tasks.

Bookending my week by saying, "Here's what we got done. Here's where we are. Are we on track? What needs to change for next week?" helps me to make sure my business is moving forward.

Model Calendar

	Mon	Tues	Wed	Thurs	Fri
8			Family/Self-Care		
9	CEO Date				CEO Date
10					
11					
12			Self-Care		
1					
2					
3					Family/Relax
4					
5	Family Night	Date Night	Ballet	Game Night	Movie Night

The Fired Up & Focused Challenge
Day 5

The next priority is the team meeting. You'll notice on my model calendar, I don't have blocks of time for admin/ops every day or week. At this stage of my business, I've got a team that's managing it for me. My team manages my inbox, schedules my social media, and helps me with pretty much anything admins/ops and customer service.

I only have to check in once through the week on such tasks during our team meeting. If it's important, they'll send me a quick message, but because we've documented systems for nearly everything behind the scenes, they are easily able to take a lot of those types of tasks off my plate.

That's something to work towards. If you don't have a team yet, you might just have a 30-minute block that's checking in for admin/ops and customer service related things instead of letting them kind of steal time from you throughout the day.

Model Calendar

	Mon	Tues	Wed	Thurs	Fri
8			Family/Self-Care		
9					
10	CEO Date				CEO Date
11	Team Meeting				
12			Self-Care		
1					
2					Family/Relax
3					
4					
5	Family Night	Date Night	Ballet	Game Night	Movie Night

The Fired Up & Focused Challenge
Day 5

After that I create blocks for client appointments. I have two big blocks of time when all of my private clients schedule to work with me. This helps me get into the flow and ensures that I'm not breaking up my content creation time with sporadic client calls.

I also run Online Masterminds calls inside Conscious Business Design and the Sweet Spot Online Mastermind. These times are consistent. By keeping them that way, there's no guesswork, people don't get confused, and we all know it's happening.

Model Calendar

	Mon	Tues	Wed	Thurs	Fri
8			Family/Self-Care		
9					
10	CEO Date				CEO Date
11	Team Meeting				
12			Self-Care		
1		Clients	Clients		
2		Clients	Clients		
3					Family/Relax
4	Online Mastermind			Online Mastermind	
5	Family Night	Date Night	Ballet	Game Night	Movie Night

The Fired Up & Focused Challenge
Day 5

Next, I create blocks of time for content creation. Content creation could be marketing related, such as writing blog posts or doing interviews. It could also be creating paid content for my Conscious Business Design or Sweet Spot Online Mastermind programs.

Not every entrepreneur will require so many hours dedicated to content creation - but if you're running an online teaching and coaching business similar to mine, you'll be amazed how much your role as CEO of your biz will become creating content for your community!

Model Calendar

	Mon	Tues	Wed	Thurs	Fri
8	Family/Self-Care				
9	CEO Date	Content Creation	Content Creation	Content Creation	CEO Date
10					
11	Team Meeting				Biz BFF Date
12	Self-Care				
1		Clients	Clients		
2					Family/Relax
3					
4	Online Mastermind			Online Mastermind	
5	Family Night	Date Night	Ballet	Game Night	Movie Night

The Fired Up & Focused Challenge
Day 5

Another crucial appointment on my calendar? A regular biz BFF date. If you don't have a biz BFF, I highly recommend that you find one. A biz BFF is like an accountability partner, a mastermind partner. Someone who gets you and can hold you up to your highest. Encourage you, cheer you on and help you when you get stuck.

I make it a point on my calendar to regularly be touching base with my biz BFFs. I'll also use this time to meet new people who could potentially be great contacts or who might be interested in supporting each others businesses. If you don't have a biz BFF, make sure you join our exclusive Fired Up and Focused community to find someone!

The final blocks of time that I schedule are for biz development and education. This is where if I have a lot of planning going on - maybe I'm mapping out a launch for a program, or I'm learning how to do something new like upgrade my copywriting skills. I've got time in my calendar so that I can work on those things bit by bit.

Model Calendar

	Mon	Tues	Wed	Thurs	Fri
8	Family/Self-Care				
9					
10	CEO Date	Content Creation	Content Creation	Content Creation	CEO Date
11	Team Meeting				Biz BFF Date
12	Self-Care				
1	Biz Dev + Education	Clients	Clients	Biz Dev + Education	
2					
3					Family/Relax
4	Online Mastermind			Online Mastermind	
5	Family Night	Date Night	Ballet	Game Night	Movie Night

The Fired Up & Focused Challenge
Day 5

I have found that having all of these blocks of time in my calendar ensures that I never get into a panic mode, worried that something suddenly is going to be missed, and I'm going to have to take an entire week to catch up, regain balance, or fill in something that went missing.

It's what allows me to make these tiny steps forward each and every day.

Take Your Biz on a CEO Date

Now that we've had a look at the model calendar fully assembled, let's go on a CEO date. This is all about stepping out of worker bee mode and getting into CEO mode. I highly encourage everyone to take their business on a CEO date on a regular basis.

Looking at your business from a high level to make sure that all of that work you're doing is getting you where you ultimately want to go... this deserves committed, focused, distraction-free time. Schedule a CEO Date weekly!

It all comes down to this: if you fail to plan, you plan to fail. This is a really well known saying for a reason. To get to your goals, you have to have a plan to get there.

There are a few different types of CEO dates depending on what level of strategic planning you're focused on.

Every year I block out one full week to brainstorm, mastermind, and plan the big projects for the calendar year ahead.

Then, each season or every quarter, I break those yearly goals down into the top one to three things we're going to create, complete, or prioritize during the next 90 Days.

One season we might be focused on getting systems worked out for all of our customer service. One season we might be focused on creating a new program. One season we might be focused on doing a lot of outgoing marketing like getting interviewed or doing guest posts.

Having these types of focuses for each season helps me get momentum in a relatively short timeframe of just a few months.

Once I have that seasonal plan, then I take it month by month and break it down. For example, if my seasonal focus was to get some outreach marketing going - I was going to do lots of interviews and lots of guest posts - then each month I'd be saying, "Well, how many places am I guest posting this month? How many places am I getting interviewed?"

I would chunk it down and give myself a tangible check-off-able goal. If I knew over the month I wanted to be interviewed five times, each week I would make sure that I was either pitching myself or getting booked for interviews so that I can meet that overall big picture goal.

Day 5:: Fired Up & Focused Challenge

1) Create your model calendar.

Download the bonus worksheet at http://www.firedupandfocused.com/book to get started. Create some sacred space for your week and you'll be able to set clearer boundaries between your personal and your work life.

2) Try it on for a week.

If you find that it's not working for you, then you need to tweak it. It may take a few months to find the right schedule for you.

3) Have your first CEO date.

Go ahead and put it into your calendar. Make a date with your business. You'll be so glad that you checked in to see how you're doing working towards those big picture priorities that you have.

Day 6:: Burning Out?
You Need a Business Savasana!

Have you ever had your best ideas in the shower? Or when you're waking up from a dream? Or during your yoga or meditation practice?

If you've ever experienced that flash of insight or maybe even finally figured out the solution to some problem during one of those moments when you've allowed your mind to just wander freely, then you've experienced what's been called the Creative Pause.

More and more creative people are finally recognizing the importance of allowing your mind some room to just be, to observe, to wander around. This is probably different from what you may be expecting from book about productivity!

Most people think that being highly productive is about always being ON; it's about doing more, about always being on task, always working on something - squeezing more on to an already overflowing plate.

What I've realized is this approach is not conducive to doing your best and most creative work. It actually can be counterproductive to creating high productivity and high performance in your business and your life.

That's where integrating a Creative Pause into your week comes in. A Creative Pause is essentially about giving your brain some white space. It's about creating a distraction free period so that your mind can wander and your subconscious can have the bandwidth it needs to come up with new creative connections.

In today's society, distraction free can be as simple as screen free. It's obvious that we are surrounded by screens 24/7. Most of us are spending eight hours a day looking at a computer and we have an iPad by our side and a phone in our pocket. We are always looking at a screen.

You don't have to do any more than walk down a busy sidewalk to realize that our entire society is obsessed with being on all the time. People don't look up and smile anymore. They're always looking down as they're tweeting or firing off an email.

When your mind is always attached to these devices, literally addicted to these devices, it's distracted from the present moment. You're not allowing yourself the space that your brain, your subconscious, needs to wander around, to sort through all of the inputs it's been taking in.

When you create this distraction free time, you're giving your brain the space it needs to start making those connections, to tie up those loose ends.

One of the best ways you can do begin experimenting with the Creative Pause is to add a mindfulness practice to your workday. I've shared a little about this with you already.

We've created a mindfulness practice is by adding a ritual to start and end your day. Another thing we've talked about is using the Pomodoro Technique, which allows you to have these short, highly focused, productive bursts of energy and then you unplug, take a break and allow your mind some breathing room.

By adding in Creative Pauses throughout your day - doing something novel or frivolous during those breaks like reading a fiction book or taking a walk - really allows your brain to relax and later come back to work refreshed and ready to be even more productive and engaged.

You can also practice mindfulness in your routine daily tasks. Just like you have those short bursts of inspiration when you're in the shower, you can have that same burst of inspiration while you're doing something like washing the dishes, folding laundry, or walking to meet your kids at the bus stop.

When you allow yourself to use those times to do what you're doing without adding more inputs your brain will have the space it needs to make those cool connections and insights.

The final way you can add a mindfulness practice is by having a physical practice. Make sure you have movement in your day - walking or running or working out or taking a yoga class or taking a dance class - without zoning out with headphones or TV, but only paying attention to what's happening in your physical body.

Be present with yourself. This type of practice allows you to drop in and get reconnected so that you come out of that practice more engaged and more aware of what's going on, the strength inside you, and the world around you.

The most amazing thing about adding even one of these mindfulness practices into your routine and allow space for the "creative pause" regularly, your subconscious goes to work for you.

You're telling your subconscious, "*We're going to shift gears. We're going to level down, power down to about 70% of our normal productiveness.*"

It allows your subconscious to find those connections, to come up with new ideas and new insights. It'll go to work for you while you're doing something effortless.

Rest is Productive

This is a concept that I learned from the amazing Danielle LaPorte. A few years back, she wrote this fabulous blog post that was about creativity, the corpse pose and what to do between projects.

Many yogis know that savasana is the pose we do at the end of our practice. We're literally laying on our backs, our arms and feet stretched out and it's the time that we use to integrate all of the work we did on the mat so that we can get up and leave the studio, leave our practice, ready to take on the day with this new sense of energy, this new sense of enthusiasm.

Many entrepreneurs don't allow themselves that integration time. We work on these big projects, we create workshops and retreats and new programs and all this content... We create this huge body of work which requires periods of highly focused energy.

Unfortunately, we start to burn ourselves out because we haven't give ourselves this space, this savasana, to integrate and process the work that we've done before we start the next thing.

The Side Effects of Productivity

When you're in that productive state, you've kind of created this bubble. Usually it means you've put something else on hold so that you can focus on doing your highest-level work. Maybe you had to put your personal life stuff on hold, you didn't get to do laundry this week or pay all of your bills and you've got to catch up on that.

Maybe you put business on hold. Maybe you just said, "I'm not going to answer my emails for the next couple of days. I'm not going to jump into all these things. I have to be really focused."

When you come out of that focused bubble, the instinct is to catch up. To catch up on life, to catch up on business. At the same time, your brain doesn't need you to jump into catching up; it needs you to power down. It needs you to rest and recharge.

If you're always on the go go go, you're kind of treating your brain like an endurance machine. The truth is, we are not machines. Your brain needs a break.

Even machines need a break. They need to be shut down. They need maintenance. If you've ever left your computer on for days and days on end, you'll see it slow down and you'll get less productivity out of it.

Your brain is the same way. If you don't give it that space to power down, then everything stops working at the optimal level.

We're also chasing that high of productivity. We're really fired up because we just finished this big thing. We have this feeling like, "Yeah! I just knocked out that to do list. I got so much done. I'm on fire!" You're ravenous, and look around you, saying, "What else can I do? What else needs to get done?"

It creates this almost manic state and you end up doing yourself a huge disservice. You'll put yourself on the fast path to burnout if you rush right into the next thing that you need to get done.

Don't jump feet first into the next big project! Your brain and body need time to rest, recoup, and rejuvenate.

Again, it's all about integration. It's about giving yourself that downtime, that rest and rejuvenation time, so that you can come back to work refreshed and bring your A-game every single day to your work, to your family, to your personal life, to everything that matters to you.

Take a Business Savasana

Create some space to unplug from your business at least one full day a week. By unplug, I actually mean unplugging. Don't do any work on the computer, don't check your business email, don't jump on to schedule some social media updates, don't use that date to catch up.

It means focusing on yourself, focusing on your self-care, focusing on your family time. This is that day a week where you can read those books you've been putting on hold. You can go see that amazing art exhibit you've been hearing about. This is time to re-engage with your life, and take a step back from your business.

Seasonal or quarterly business savasana retreats are good for the soul. These could be three or four days where you literally step away from the day to day in your business. These could be the regular times where you take your family on a mini-vacation. These could be solo-retreats. Go check out those yoga classes you've heard about, or book yourself into a bed and breakfast and pamper yourself for a few days.

It could even be time where you get your friends together -- whether they're personal friends and you're just wanting to reconnect and have fun, or business BFFs who want to get together and just support each other, encourage each other.

That last example is quite different, but I find that when I have those business BFFs together for a business savasana, we all come back really excited and lit up about the new connections we've made in our business.

Commit to REAL vacation time every year. I'd encourage you to block off at least 2 weeks a year. I'm not looking for an entire month off at once since I've built in relaxing, rejuvenating time on a regular basis. But, many entrepreneurs forget that we need space, we need breaks, and we end up working years on end without having a real vacation.

Make sure you're blocking out at least one to two weeks a year where you're not in your business. It makes sure a profound difference when you're able to come back and get back to work with this restored mindset.

Day 6:: Fired Up & Focused Challenge!

It's time to get into inspired action and make time for mindfulness.

1) What creative pause are you going to add to work today?

Here's some of my favorites:

- Going to lunch by yourself. Not with a book, not with your iPhone. Just going to lunch, sitting there, tasting the food and watching/observing the people around you

- Going on a long walk in nature. Not with a headset, not with a podcast. Just you in nature, listening and being aware of what's happening around you

- A little bit more silly or frivolous: sitting on the back porch and just blowing bubbles. Something that's fun and lighthearted really allows me to get out of my normal serious state.

2) Schedule your first Business Savasana.

I recommend starting with that one day a week where you're unplugged from your business. If that means you need to hide your cell phone or take the apps off of so that you can have a Saturday or a Sunday just to do something for you, do it.

This is a great time to read a fiction book that you've wanted to read; to go to the movies; to volunteer for a non-profit that you love; to go on a solo retreat. Get out of your business and get back into being engaged with your life.

You've accomplished a TON this week - now it's time to have some FUN!

Day 7:: Your Definition of Success

Is there any topic that triggers working women more than the question of having it all?

It's a phrase that is loaded with emotion.

Mostly shame, guilt, and anxiety as women attempt to not only create a successful career or business… but also be the perfect wife {who always wants sexy time with her hubby} with the perfect children {who are not only perfectly behaved, but little prodigies who you also happen to home school and coach all the teams for}, living in the Pinterest perfectly decorated {and organized and never messy} homes, cooking from scratch organic + gluten free feasts every night while snapping {carefully curated} carefree Instagram pics to document {aka show off} your perfect life.

Oh - and don't forget that we've gotta throw in the perfect body too. And you and your entire perfect family adores signing up for every race that comes through your town.

All while you manage to effortlessly run a multiple 6-or-7 figure business in just a few hours a week.

'Cause we don't have enough pressure. AMIRIGHT?

Like most women growing up in the 80s and 90s, I was raised with a generation of girls who were told that we could grow up to have it all.

We could go to college. Break through the glass ceilings in corporate America. Bring home the bacon and fry in up in the pan.

We could achieve ANYTHING.

And so we did.

More women than ever before are graduating college, scooping up Master's degrees, and becoming doctors, lawyers, and professionals. We have incredible women in powerful positions, sharing how we can Lean In to become leaders, executives, and CEOs in our industries.

And yet, despite all of the progress women have made in the workplace over the last few decades, it's simply not enough.

We're still struggling to close the wage gap.

We're fighting for our rights to paid maternity leave.

We're still underrepresented as CEOs, executives, and leaders in every industry.

It explains why more and more women are breaking free from the old paradigm of climbing a corporate ladder to follow their own path into entrepreneurship.

After all, if the rules of the game aren't working, isn't it time to just change the rules?

Last year, I had the honor of speaking to the US Chamber of Commerce Center for Women in Business. Afterwards, I spent nearly 2 hours talking with women who want to create their own version of success but were struggling in this old paradigm.

As I talked with these amazing women entrepreneurs from around the US, I realized that too often, the only measure of success we focus on is dolla dolla bills. While over 88% of women entrepreneurs never break the 6-figure mark in their biz... the honest truth is money is only ONE metric of success.

And don't get me wrong - a profitable business is a non-negotiable for business success. Unless you wanna have an expensive hobby, this business has gotta pay the bills!

But when we're only focused on the money, instead of creating a business that loves us back, we find ourselves in an abusive relationship with a business that demands 100% of our time and energy, not to mention putting us on the fast track to burnout {and according to most research, 80% of new businesses crash and burn within the first couple of years}.

How can we better set ourselves up for long-term success?

You've gotta define what success means, to you.

Without spending time answering this crucial question, we set ourselves up for disappointment when someone else's version of success just doesn't fit us, our lifestyle, or our family.

Clarity around your definition of success is incredibly empowering. It becomes a filter for decision making, helping you to quickly assess if an opportunity is a shiny object or a gold mine. It helps you to make space for what really matters in your life. And it becomes a tool you can use to strategically plan the trajectory of your business.

Day 7:: Fired Up & Focused Challenge!

Let's review some key areas of your life and business to create your unique definition of success.

Part 1:: Your Life + Lifestyle

This might sound completely backwards... but I've found over and over again that it you don't makes space for what matters most to you in your life, you'll struggle to find space for it at all.

Ask yourself::

- If you could plan an ideal 'regular-day', what would it look like?

- What about an entire ideal week?

- How much time would you spend working? How much time do you take off?

- What are your top 3 lifestyle non-negotiables {as in, you MUST have these in order to feel happy + fulfilled}?

- If you could upgrade 3 things in your current lifestyle in the next 90 days, what would you upgrade?

Part 2:: Your Family + Friends

Relationships are so important to women entrepreneurs… but too often we get so wrapped up in our businesses, that we struggle to have quality time with our own families, friends, and loved ones.

Ask yourself::

- Who are your most important relationships in your life, right now {top 5 at least!}?

- What does quality time with these people look like for you?

- How often do you want to have quality time with these people in your life?

- How often do you want to have a date night {or getaway!} with your partner?

- How often do you make time for friends?

Part 3:: Your Health + Wellbeing

Raising my hand right here because this is the area I often put LAST! But having a clear picture of what you'd like to experience in your health, wellbeing, and body is essential to making time to care for yourself!

Ask yourself::

- Are you satisfied with your current state of health + wellbeing?

- What does a healthy body look + feel like, to you?

- What would you like your self-care to look like each day, week, and month?

- Are you making time each day to move your body {aka exercise?}?

- How do you nourish your body each day?

Part 4:: Your Creativity + Self-Expression

We entrepreneurs are creative beings! We love to learn, grow, try new things, and dabble with new hobbies… and spending time on other interests will help you be more refreshed + creative in your business!

Ask yourself::

- What do you do for fun?

- What interests would you like to learn more about?

- Are there any classes you wish you could take?

- What hobbies do you wish you had time to pursue {*hint* make some time!}?

Part 5:: Your Personal Growth + Spirituality

When you're investing energy into filling your own love-tank, you'll feel more grounded and empowered each and every day in your life and business.

Ask yourself::

- How much 'quiet time' do you need each day to sit with your thoughts?

- What mindfulness practices do you want to start {meditation, journaling, yoga}?

- What are your favorite uplifting books and blogs to read?

- What helps you to stay inspired and focused in your life and business?

- How often do you need to feel your soul + spirit each week?

Day 8:: End Email Overload

So far, we have looked at how successful CFOs approach their work week. For many solopreneurs, this is 180-degree flip from how we usually spend our time, running our businesses on default instead of by design.

Our goal is to continue to shift towards acting as the true CEOs of our business, spending more of our time and energy on the highest impact areas - the areas of our business that get results, drive the bottom line, help us serve more people, and ultimately allow us to do more of what we love {and less busy work!}.

Before we dive into higher level areas like marketing and business development, first we've gotta streamline and systematize the task areas that keep the day-to-day running smoothly in our businesses. Over the next few days, these are strategies that you can implement right away and begin to see results in each of these five core task areas of your business.

The Novel in Your Inbox

Do you remember back in the early 90s there was a really adorable rom-com with Meg Ryan and Tom Hanks called You've Got Mail? The characters were so excited every time they got that little notification on their computer with this adorable British accent saying, "*You've got mail!*"

They were thrilled someone was emailing them. It was new and it was a fun thing for them to be communicating in this way.

Fast forward 20-odd years and it's simply not like that anymore. Email overwhelm is a very real problem. In fact, it's one of the biggest problems that every working adult faces - regardless of if you work for yourself or someone else. Everyone is dealing with email overwhelm.

In fact, did you know that you'll write a novel this year? That's right. Research is showing that the average person is spending 13 hours a week answering emails. That's 650 hours a year and over 166 pages of emails written. That's *The Great Gatsby.*

It is crazy how much time we're spending in the inbox. And I expect solopreneurs spend much more time than the average worker.

Your Inbox is Someone Else's To Do List.

Most people start their work day by sitting down and opening their email. That's how they decide what they're going to work on first. It's someone else saying, *"Hey, what I need from you is more important than what you need to get started with."*

Stop and ask yourself who's running the show. Who's the CEO of this place anyway? Is their to do list more important than yours as the CEO of your business? I don't think so! It's time to end the email overload and begin to get more stuff done.

I'm going to start by sharing my favorite strategies and walk you through a process to clear the clutter, clean out the inbox, and give you a system to follow so that you're not bombarded with email every day.

Boundaries are Good For Business

Setting boundaries is so crucial in email and in life. If you don't have boundaries in place, then you're at the beck and call of everyone: your clients, your assistants, your team, your mom emailing you in the middle of your workday.

Everyone thinks that that moment they hit send, they're going to get an instant reply from you. That's not possible, and not even reasonable. We have to have some boundaries in mind.

We can start by looking at what responses people actually need from me right away. Chances are you're worried that someone needs information that they are not finding themselves. They need to how I get to your yoga studio, or what classes you are teaching this week, or how they can log into your webinar.

These are regular FAQ types that are coming in. If they search hard enough, they probably would find the answer, but because most of us are looking for convenience we all think, "It will just be easier to email them. Surely they'll send us a response right away because, like me, they're looking at their inbox 24/7."

This is one of the easiest types of hassles that we can automate by creating an FAQ auto-responder.

I learned this from my friend, Alexandra Franzen. It's become a great strategy to answer the simple questions instantly without having to personally address each one.

You simply set up a vacation auto responder in your email provider that contains the answers to the top questions {maybe 3 - 5 questions} that people often email in to ask. You don't have to respond to them. Those questions landing in your inbox now get answered automatically. It's amazing!

And it frees up so much bandwidth for you to be free from answering those same little nitty-gritty detail type of emails.

Create an FAQ AutoResponder

This is so simple to do. You simply write up the email then load into your vacation reply option in your email. I usually start by saying something like,

"Hey, there. I received your email and will respond as quickly as possible -- usually within two business days. I do my best to take off for weekends. But, in the meantime, here's a rundown of the topics that most people email me about. You might find your answer right here."

Following this simple intro, I provide answers to my top three to five questions.

The key here is to let people know what to expect aka how long it takes you to respond. I always find it's important to tell them that I take off for the weekends, otherwise people really do think that they can send you an email on Friday afternoon and that you're going to spend your weekend responding to them.

The type of FAQs you have depend on your business, but there are some general commonalities:

- How can I find out more about working with you? {Provide a link to your Work With Me page.}

- How can I interview you for this thing? {Link them to your Media page.}

- How can I find out more about whatever else you have going on? {Link them to your blog or provide a link to your best free content.}

You can put those FAQs below the intro and change it up on a monthly basis based on what's going on in your business.

While some email questions and content can be predicted and covered by an FAQ auto-responder, once you have clients and colleagues, you're going to want to give them genuine, quality, dedicated communication. Remember - an amazing customer experience is what keeps them coming back for more!

Set the expectation of a 24-48 hour response time for your VIPs.

These are the people who are your private clients/highest level paying clients - or personal contacts that you might be working with and need to respond to quickly, such as your team, coaches, business BFFs, or other colleagues that you work with on a regular basis.

The most important thing about managing your VIPs is letting them know what to expect. If your private clients think that they're going to hear from you within an hour, they're going to be really frustrated when it takes a day.

I set these expectations up front. When I take on a new private client, I let them know, *"You're a VIP client for me. If your email hits my inbox, I will make sure to respond to you as quickly as possible. Usually within 24 hours unless it's the weekend. With that in mind, make sure you plan accordingly in case you need me to look at something."*

Setting those expectations means clear understanding going forward, and prevents frustration on either side.

Create Responses in Advance

Along the same lines of the FAQ auto-responder is what I call Response in Advance. Have you ever heard the saying, *"The fortune is in the follow up?"* The truth is, a lot of us are getting opportunities all the time and if we don't respond right away, we're going to miss out.

Maybe it's happened to you. You've checked your emails, you had a request for more information from a potential client and you start to dash off this super fast - and maybe not so well thought out email - with as much information as possible to hopefully get them to work with you.

Or, maybe because you've been checking your inbox when you weren't planning on writing a thoughtful email, you said, *"Oh, I'll wait for a little bit until I have some more time."*

Or, maybe you wrote the best response ever - something amazing that answered all the questions, was super thoughtful - and you felt like you nailed it. They're surely going to become a new client. Then you don't hear back from them.

It starts to feel like all of that time you spent writing out this very detailed response is wasted. Unfortunately, this is the life of an entrepreneur. Not everything pans out, not everyone becomes a client.

But we can still take advantage of technology available to us to help us respond thoughtfully to people without recreating the wheel each time.

When opportunity knocks, you want to be ready! You do that by pre-writing all your answers to the top questions that you are asked so that you can respond quickly and professionally.

What types of questions do you want to have these pre-written responses for?

1. How can I work with you?

The most important response you should have ready to go telling them what the process is and what they need to do next.

2. Which program is a better fit for me?

Maybe you have a group program and a one-on-one program. Let them know the pros and cons of each and where they can find out more.

3. What are your rates?

I rarely answer this question right up front because it's important for me to get clearer on what they actually need first. Otherwise, they might just be price shopping. Having a well thought out email response to this to redirect their focus and get clearer on what they're actual needs are will ensure that you're having a much better conversation that's more likely to lead to a new client.

4. Are you interested in being interviewed or contributing?

Usually, people will send out that simple of a question and, honestly, I won't say yes or no until I learn more about it. Having something that lets them know exactly what my expectations are, what I'm saying yes to right now, what I'm saying no to, what topics I talk about and links them to my media page to learn more about what I love to talk about is where I point them.

5. Can I pick your brain or will you work for free?

These types of emails are usually coming in the request of answering a little question. They're asking for a piece of advice. If you're getting a lot of those, maybe you need to have a thoughtful question response that says, *"I'd love to talk with you more about that. Here's how you can learn about booking a session with me."*

Having those types of responses ready to go will really reduce your stress and help you get the answers that they need as quickly as possible. You just pre-write them and save them as canned responses in your email that you can pull up instantly.

The difference between this strategy and the FAQ auto-responder?

These are more personal responses so they have better odds of getting a conversation going. The trick is still having answers prepared for questions you know you'll get, so you can respond quickly without re-creating the wheel over and over again.

Most everyone else can fall under the 1-2x weekly email responses.

Occasionally, you'll get requests from people who aren't clients. They're not urgent requests and, honestly, they're probably not ready to become clients right away.

Some are the pick-your-brain emails. People just want your advice. You don't necessarily want to put them off, but at the same time, you don't want to set a precedent for responding to these all the time - you can have free content, but your time can't be available for free.

Brand building emails fit into the 1-week response category too. When someone wants you to contribute a guest post or participate in their telesummit, interview series, etc... They're things that get you exposure at some point, but they're not urgent and don't demand your immediate email reply.

I group all these and sit down to answer them in about a 30-minute block once a week. Yeah, I could fire off a response every single day, but the more that you group like with like, the easier it is to manage it.

Remember - not every email requires a response. There might be some emails in your inbox that you just don't need to answer. They're not asking a question, you aren't having to confirm anything and it might just be like a, "Just so you know…" type of thing. If that's the case, delete, archive it, get it out of your vision so that you're not feeling dragged down by it.

Just Say No to Notifications

The next step to manage email overload is to turn off all the notifications. Your email inbox is not a leash. You are not a Pavlovian dog that is trained to open a message every time your device pings or vibrates on your desk.

Unless your phone number is unlisted, no one will email you with anything so urgent and critical that it demands you jump to respond. Shut off the notifications and save yourself the anxiety.

First things first, tackle social media notifications. That's right, log into all your social accounts and turn off every notification. You do not need an email in your inbox if somebody replies to you. You do not need an email in your inbox if somebody has a direct message. All of that stuff is taking up bandwidth and we need to free that up.

Next, the email notifications. You do not need to be interrupted by your own inbox when you're doing your highest level CEO work. You know that ping just begs for you to click it. Take away that distraction by turning off all the notifications.

Same thing with your phone. You do not need to be told when emails are hitting your inbox. Just turn off all the notifications. Go in there and adjust your settings. It frees up so much mental energy.

Already you should start feeling more freedom!

Clear the Inbox Clutter

Your inbox is - if it's anything like mine - full. Some messages came from places you legitimately subscribed to; that's cool. I get it; I subscribe for all sorts of newsletters. I'm always learning from other people's content, other information, but I don't need to read it all the minute it lands in my inbox.

If you're finding that your inbox is clogged up with newsletters that you think you want to read, but never get around to, then right now, it's just becoming a distraction. Maybe it's time to unsubscribe from anything that you haven't opened in the last three months. You can always go back and re-subscribe.

Please do not hang onto newsletters because you're worried that you're going to miss out. If you're not getting enough value from them to open in the last three months, it's time to let it go.

Another option is to use a tool like Unroll.me. It's one of my favorite tools that basically goes in your inbox, says, "Here's all the newsletters you're subscribed to. Do you want a daily digest or a weekly digest?" Then it diverts them all into this single newsletter for you to digest once a day or week.

It's amazing! You instantly have less potential for distractions during your work day, and way less inbox items to sort through. I set my Unroll Me digest to deliver at the end of the day and can just skim through it before switching gears to reading an evening book. It doesn't take up my valuable business CEO time or distract me from my to-do list.

One-Touch Your Email

This is my system for getting through my inbox really, really quickly.

Do not start your day with email.

We're going to start our days by looking at our must-do-tomorrow list from the previous workday so our time and focus goes to the most important task. Period.

Instead, choose 2-3 times that you manage your email each day. How you approach this is up to you. Currently, I only check my inbox about once a day, twice if things are really busy. But, I'm letting my assistant and team handle it as much as possible {and I've given them permission to kick me out of the inbox}. That's the goal.

Your email really is something that an assistant can help manage. They can send out responses using your Respond in Advance answers, and make sure that you're only dealing with the most important emails. It's really great to be able to have that out of your mental bandwidth zone so that you can focus on creating the highest level value in your business.

If you're only going to choose two to three times, what I've done is I've just programmed a little alarm in my phone that says, " *11:00 AM. Check my email.*" *"4:00 PM. Check my email.*" I know I'll do it, because it's the only notification I get!

Now on to the "one-touch" email game. This comes from the David Allen approach of managing things. It's about reminding yourself of the simplest options you have; you have four options when you open an email::

1. You can respond to it.

2. You can boomerang it. This is a really cool plugin you can get for Gmail which essentially hides the email and then just brings it back into your inbox within a certain period of time. Let's say, you don't have to really follow up with them for two months. You just boomerang it and say, "I want to get this back in two months so I remember to follow up," and it takes it out of your inbox so it's not just clutter.

3. You can delete it.

4. You can archive it. It's one of the reasons I love Google Apps for Biz, just because I can pretty much archive everything. I don't worry that I'm going to delete something important.

Day 8:: Fired Up and Focused Challenge!

Now it's time to get into inspired action. Here's your quick checklist to manage your email inbox.

- Create your FAQ auto responder.

- Write your first response in advance. You save it as a canned response in your inbox. If you're not sure what to start with, I highly recommend going ahead and telling the universe that you are ready for more requests from potential clients and respond to the question, "How can I work with you?"

- Turn off all of those pesky notifications that are clogging up your inbox.

- Unsubscribe and roll up all of those newsletters so that they don't become a distraction.

- Get in the habit of one-touching your inbox.

Day 9:: Experience is Everything

I was dealing with a neck injury a few years ago and I wanted a yoga therapist to help me figure out how to start healing and avoid re-injury when getting back into my regular practice.

I was struggling to find someone local to me here in Richmond, Virginia, so I started looking online and asking for recommendations, and finally found someone who could work with me via Skype. I was so excited. I ended up signing up to work with her for four sessions over two months, a $600 package. It wasn't cheap. This was a high end service, and much higher than I regularly paid for a private yoga session.

When we started working together, I had some great results. I got some great tools, I knew how to modify my practice so that I wouldn't get injured again, the pain level on my neck and shoulders went down dramatically.

But I didn't sign up to be a regular client.

What happened? Why not if I got the results I was looking for?

The truths is, even though those sessions were great - she was a very knowledgeable teacher - there were a lot of things happening between our sessions that made it challenging to work with her.

We had a lot of issues getting on the same page about scheduling, about what time zone the scheduling was happening in, about rescheduling on her end and just inconsistent days and times. Monday one week, Friday a couple after that, it was very confusing and inconvenient for me as a busy mama and entrepreneur.

There were even two times where I was sitting there in front of Skype, ready to go, thinking we had an appointment and then I would get an email from her later realizing that she had missed the session or had the wrong time zone.

As a client, this is extremely frustrating and it's really important to understand that as a teacher, a coach, a heart-centered service provider, that every time you're working with someone, the relationship doesn't just include the actual time you're spending present with them. It's all the little touches in between that make a difference between someone who is just a one-time client, and someone who becomes a raving fan; somebody who loves working with you and wants to continue working with you because they're having such a great experience and they feel so cared for.

Customer Experience Goes Beyond Customer Service

Customer service is just the entry fee for being in business. Experience is all about really taking care of your people. When you have the best clients, who are telling your friends and their family/colleagues about you, it's because you've gone out of your way to have a mind-blowing experience.

The reason people talk is because you stood out from everyone else who hasn't taken the time… and you can create an amazing experience in a very strategic and simple way; a way that you can rinse and repeat, do over and over again without spinning your wheels.

Customer Experience Checklist

It all starts with having a basic customer experience checklist. I'm going to walk through one example built for people who work one-on-one. You can take and adapt this if you're working in groups or another format with your clients. It can work for you whether you're a yoga teacher or a Pilates instructor or a life coach or a nutritionist or other heart-centered service provider. This is a great starting point for you.

Step 1:: Send out a new client agreement and invoice.

When someone confirms that they're ready to work with you, send out your client agreement and, along with that, an invoice. Set the expectations; let them know what they're signing up for, what the boundaries are, what they're getting, and what their end of the bargain is.

You're also sending out a request to get paid. Now, it could be an invoice, it could be a link to pay online. We're going to kind of use "invoice" interchangeably for that.

Step 2:: Schedule all new client sessions.

The client agreement has been signed and the invoice has been paid. Now they need to get an appointment scheduled. They should already have a good idea of your availability from your agreement among other things, so this should lock in easily. Don't compromise your time or your business to be flexible - stay strong in your commitment to your model calendar.

Step 3:: Send new client intake questionnaire or new client packet.

You probably need to send them some sort of intake questionnaire. I love having one as a coach and mentor because it helps me to get on the same page with them and plan where to start even before our first session.

Step 4:: Send appointment reminders.

These are so important; they show foresight, caring, and preparedness. Let them know the hour before or day before they have a session coming up, so they can feel ready.

Then you rinse and repeat. It seems pretty basic, right? It is pretty simple and manageable, but you might risk a bad experience if your checklist is not set up correctly.

Some people overly complicate their customer service checklist. While it might be easy for you to send them a PDF with a request to print, sign, and scan... your client might feel like it's a lot of hoops to jump through to work with you.

This is a huge stumbling block I see for a lot of people. They're asking people to go through way too many steps to just say, "*Yes, I'm ready to get started.*"

Always look for the path of least resistance. *High-end service providers make it EASY to work with them by setting up the best tools and systems in advance.* You can get tools to help clients sign electronically. No printing, scanning, faxing required.

You can determine your schedule and set your availability on the same days at the same times, week after week. No awful email threads bouncing back and forth for the sake of being flexible {you're not a doormat here - you're the expert they just hired!}.

You can make it easy to pay you instantly via PayPal or Stripe. People are so used to clicking to get what they want these days, online payment services are the best way to go.

It's all about making it EASY to work with you. If you're doing all this the old-fashioned way and trying to wait until you're in person or do it all via email, you're going to end up with a lot of back and forth, overwhelm, and time wasted. Neither you nor any of your clients want to work that way!

If you haven't set up a customer experience checklist and process, you're not only wasting time but money. In my experience, just from time tracking my team, I know that if we're manually doing all of these things for all five of my private clients - which is the max I ever take at a time - without a system in place then it would easily take us two hours a month per client. That means 10 hours a month. Consider that an assistant will run you anywhere from $20 to 25 an hour, that's $200 a month spent on administrative costs.

What if you don't have a team?

You've got to consider what your time is worth. It's still going to take you that two hours per client, except instead of costing you maybe an assistant's rate of $20 an hour, you're paying yourself - or wanting to pay yourself - closer to $100 an hour. That expense has really gone up. Now you've got to generate $1000 extra a month so that you can cover your administrative time. Crazy, right? We don't want to be spending our time here.

We could also be losing money if we're using a ton of different tools. If we're using four, five, six different tools that don't talk to each other, that'll add up. It's $10 here and $25 here and $50 here. Suddenly, we've got this hodgepodge of tools that don't create an integrated system.

Streamline Your Customer Experience

What does it look in your business when you've developed a streamlined, systematized customer experience?

If you're doing this the easy way, then you are getting new clients much more easily. You've made it effortless for them to say yes, to sign up, to pay and to work with you. You've made it easy to send out those automated appointment reminders. It's all working for you behind the scenes.

You're making it easy if the invoices are going out on schedule and sending reminders when people don't pay them on time. This is so crucial. It ensures that you're getting paid and that they're holding up their end of the bargain.

Finally, you're doing this the easy way if there is an integrated system. If someone's calendar changes, if you need to move things around, everyone can quickly see the new schedule updates. If something comes up for them and they need to shift the terms of your agreement, you can adjust how many sessions they have left. All your notes and communication for each client should be easy to find in one place.

Make It Easy to Get Paid!

Probably, one of my favorite things about having a fully integrated system like that is that it's easy to get paid. This is a big question and another roadblock I see a lot of entrepreneurs creating for themselves.

55% of small businesses don't accept credit cards. We know that 66% of all transactions are paid with plastic - credit or debit; it's all the same in this context.

People are not carrying cash and they're not carrying checkbooks. People want to log in online to pay their bills. People want to book their spot in your workshop using their debit card or their credit card.

I am a walking testament to this. The only time I make absolutely sure to have cash is when I need to pay $2 to cross the toll bridge on my way to my parent's house. I use my debit or credit card for everything and I'm always amazed when I show up somewhere that they're not accepted.

In fact, it's been shown over and over again that if you set up either an online payment system or accept credit cards, suddenly you've removed barriers to work with you. You let people pay you more easily and chances are, your business is going to increase and cover the cost of those fees with ease.

Day 9:: Fired Up & Focused Challenge!

It's time to get into inspired action. I'd love for you to take a few moments and outline the process of a new client checklist.

1:: What does that customer experience checklist look like for you?

Do you need an agreement? Do you need an invoice? Do you need appointment reminders? Questionnaires? Do you need anything else that will make the process as easy as possible for them and nothing will drop through the cracks.

This is so huge. Just creating the system -- having even just a checklist -- will ensure that the overall experience goes up dramatically. Suddenly, people are raving about you and can't wait to tell their friends and family about how awesome it is to work with you.

2:: Next, how can you simplify the process and make it even easier?

Can you go from a lot of different tools that you're using to one? Can you try using an online scheduling tool so that you're not doing the email back and forth? Even just one upgrade in this process will create a great experience for your clients.

3:: Finally, how can you make it easier to pay you?

I highly recommend, again, getting something like PayPal or Stripe or Square. Those are lifesavers. They make it so easy for them to take care of those invoices, to pay you and to get started working together. Let's make it simple so that more clients can't wait to work with you.

Day 10:: Steal This System

Over the last few days we've been honing in on how we can start moving towards a model where we, as successful CEOs, spend our time working on the big picture, highest value tasks and projects.

But before we get on to the fun CEO level work, first we've got to simplify, streamline, and systematize our administrative, operations, and customer service tasks.

These are the types of tasks that take up most of the day for new entrepreneurs. This is the busy work. This is where we feel that we are getting bogged down in our business, and our business is running us instead of us the other way around.

By now, you should feel pretty amazing that you have some great tools and strategies at your disposal so that you can begin to experience less busy work.

Systems Equal Freedom

It all starts by saying yes to systems. Systems equal freedom. It's hard to believe. It sounds like they're just a boring thing that only huge big corporations ever need to worry about.

The truth is even solopreneurs need systems, especially if we're going to start freeing up time in our work week so that we can focus on that higher level CEO level tasks.

Why do systems equal freedom?

First, systems free up your time. When you have things systematized you become more efficient. When you are able to get through those things quickly, even if you are completely solo and you don't have any support, then you can get those things crossed off your list faster so you can shift your time and attention to what is really going to move your business forward.

Second, systems prevent mistakes. If you've ever gotten frustrated with these busy type of work tasks and then the wrong link went out to somebody, or the wrong date goes on an appointment reminder... These mistakes tend to happen when there's not clear checklist in place. There is nothing to help you make sure that you are getting it done right the first time, so you end up cleaning up messes too often in your biz.

Finally, systems help you to stay on task. They help you to know exactly what step needs to happen next and then the step after that and then the step after that to achieve the desired result that you are looking for. This is really, really important. If you want to be more efficient where you are getting more done in less time, then you want to know exactly what you need to be doing.

Systems Help You Clone Yourself

This is one of the areas where I hear people say, "Well, I think I need an assistant, but I don't know what I want them to do."

The reason they don't know what they want them to do is because they don't have a checklist in place for any area of their business. They are worried that they are going to have to sit here and spend all this time training someone.

If you ever want to grow your business, you basically have two options::

1. You have to get faster and more efficient at doing all these types of tasks, or

2. You have to pass them off to a team member before you become a bottleneck in your business.

Once you have a system in place, you can speed up the process and bring someone else into your business to check off that list.

You'll start to grow because your time is spent adding value to your business.

If you're running a business that you hope to sell one day or pass off to somebody, the ship will have already been built. With systems in place, they are much more likely to say, "Yes, I will buy your business from you," and someone can more easily step on and manage that business.

It's a huge value-add to have a business that runs like a well-oiled machine. It makes that business very valuable and turns it into a true asset {aka something that will continue to grow in value for you}.

I love, I love, I love systems. It's about not reinventing the wheel every time you have to do a new project; when you do a thing once, record your steps and lessons to pass on for the next time.

Finding Opportunities for Systems in Your Business

What systems do you have or do you need? Like I said, a system is basically a checklist. It's just something to make sure that all the steps are followed and that nothing gets left behind.

There are usually, a lot, a lot, a lot of small little individual tasks that make up an entire process you have to go through. Having a clear process in place, a clear checklist in place, makes it easy for you to stay on task, to get it done and get the results you are looking for.

Take a moment here and note to yourself - what are three systems that you know you need checklist for right now?

I recommend thinking about the things that you are doing on a regular basis. Things that you want to get done faster; things that have a lot of moving parts and anything that could be passed off to an assistant as quickly as possible. All that they are waiting on is for you to tell them exactly what needs to be done.

Create a Systems Hub

The next piece in creating systems is to keep it all in one place. We use Google Drive. We use Google Docs for all of our internal biz systems.

You could use Google, you could use Word Documents, you could use PowerPoint, you could use Evernote, or a project management tool like Asana or Basecamp or Trello. All of those things work equally well. The point is to have one place where you are saving everything.

Now, you've already noted which systems you are going to create so go ahead and create that folder, that place where you are going to save them, and save a document for each system.

Don't fill it out yet, just save a draft document. Once you have that document or folder ready to go, then I want to walk you through creating your first system. Again, a system is just a checklist that you put together so that anyone can follow all the steps.

A fast way to create that checklist is to use a tool like Jing or Screener. These are screen capture programs that allow you to record yourself while you are going through something on your computer. The best part about having a video that shows you going through all the steps is then you can train someone else how to do it and even pass the video off to them so they can create the checklist for you.

Steal This System:: Blog Checklist

Let's take a look at an example system. This is one that I follow each time I write a blog post on RachealCook.com, or the TheYogipreneur.com because, really, there are a lot of steps we go through to make sure that the post gets written, published and promoted.

1. Write blog post. Pretty straightforward, right?

2. Create a featured image. This is the image that shows up near the top of the post with a headline. It shows up on the main blog page, where there are little excerpts for each individual post, so I usually like to have an image that is branded, where I actually go and do something like PicMonkey or Canva and put the title of the post overlaid on top of a piece of stock photography.

3. Include 1-3 Click to Tweets. One of my favorite plug-ins called Click to Tweet where you can literally have a tweetable in the middle of your blog posts. It's a great way to boost engagement. I want to make sure that each post has 1-3 of those.

4. Write Newsletter Blurb. I share an excerpt from my post and then direct my readers to the full blog post. Going ahead and writing it while I am wrapping up the post just simplifies everything and it makes sure that it is ready to go.

5. Schedule Newsletter. Then, I go ahead and upload and schedule the newsletter so that it is going out for whatever day it is scheduled for.

6. Write Social Media Posts. I will wrap it all up by getting my social media posts ready. Sometimes that means also making images sized for social media; images that fit on Pinterest are different images that fit on Facebook are different images that fit on Twitter. We make sure that we have several different posts for each blog post. That way we are driving traffic back to the website.

7. Schedule Social Media Posts. Finally, we upload and schedule those social media posts in our scheduling tool called, Edgar, which we absolutely love.

This is the process I go through to write, to promote, to publish each and every blog post and make sure that we get traffic and then that we are sharing it with people on a regular basis.

Steal This System:: New Client Process

Another example could be a new coaching client. This could work with pretty much any other type of service-based business where you want to accept people by invitation only.

1. Receive new client application. Let's say you have an application on your website. I love having an application because it allows you to screen people for fit before you accept them.

2. Decline Application? If so, then I send them a kind and thoughtful decline via canned response. Often, for me, it's just because I'm booked out that I have to decline people. Sometimes it is a wait list. Usually I go to this if I know I am going to take on new people within a reasonable timeframe -- like less than a month or two. Then I will let them know, "*I am actually full up until this date. If you are interested I can go ahead and get you on the wait list and we will come back and revisit later.*"

3. Accept Application? If it is a yes, then I send them an email saying,

"Hey, I'd love to talk with you about working with me inside this mentorship program. Let's set aside 20 minutes so that we can make sure it is a 100% perfect fit. Here is a link to my online scheduling tool. I usually do these appointments on Fridays at this time. Go ahead and get booked in my calendar and then we'll talk about what working together for the next 6 months would look like."

4. Potential Client Interview. Then the interview is scheduled where we can have 20 minutes to make sure we definitely both want to work together. We get to know each other. They can ask me questions and I can ask them questions. It's great.

5. Accept New Client. Once we've completed the interview and agreed that it's a perfect fit, then I can go ahead and send them the agreement and the invoice. I do all of the scheduling, all of the agreements, all of the invoices through Satori App. It makes my life so, so simple.

6. Send New Client Packet. Once I get the agreement and the invoice back, then I send them the workbook for our first session. That first session is a deep dive and the more information they can give me in advance, the faster of a start we can get off to in our sessions. I want to get directly to the heart of the matter as quickly as we can.

7. Send New Client Welcome Gift. This doesn't have to be anything huge but it's amazing the impact a thank you note or a fresh bouquet of flowers will make on your clients getting excited to work together!

That's what a new client checklist looks like for it. It's pretty straightforward. The most important part is making sure that we've thanked them. This is one little touch that I think a lot of people miss out on, but will really make your experience take off. Finding a fun way to make these little personal touches really does make a difference.

Day 10:: Fired Up & Focused Challenge!

First, choose the three systems that you're going to map out. These are probably things you want to get off of your plate pretty quickly. You want to make sure they are being handled the same way every single time so that your clients have a consistent experience.

1)

2)

3)

Where are you creating your Systems Hub? Wherever you plan to save it, go ahead and save drafts for each of the three systems you plan to map out.

Begin writing checklists for each of those systems. It's totally okay to steal the checklists from the ones that I just gave you if you found them helpful as a baseline and as a starting point.

Bonus: Write out your systems as you are actually going through the process. As you are going through your own workday, if you realize that this is something that you should be documenting, go ahead and take the extra minute to write out all of the steps each step of the way so that you have a completed system ready to go.

Day 11:: Begin With The End In Mind

We've dug deep into streamlining, systematizing and simplifying some of these core task areas in your business that you have to manage as a business owner.

But now that we've really optimized your admin and ops, we've up-leveled your customer experience... what we've really done is created some space for you! Now you've got more quality time and energy that has freed up so that you can now step into being the CEO of your business.

It's exciting, right? Getting out of the daily grind so that you can actually think about the big picture! This is what most entrepreneurs live for - the big ideas!

The challenge is that once you start thinking about the big picture, you start feeling overloaded by ideas. There are so many great ways that you can grow your business, that you can serve your community, that you can get the word out there about what you do.

You can go online, you can work in person locally, you can work one-on-one, you can work in groups, you can host workshops, you can speak on the stage, you can offer retreats, and you can write a book. You can podcast or write newsletters or blog or become a contributor somewhere or be interviewed.

Then there's more and more noise coming at all of us from the entire business expert community telling us what you should be doing. You should be everywhere. You should be blogging. You should be running a podcast. You should be setting your business up in this way.

It's completely overwhelming. I get it. I hear you. I've been there.

It's enough to make you kind of freeze up because you're terrified that you're going to make the wrong decision. Or the opposite happens and you go for everything at once. Instead of giving something a real chance at getting roots and growing, you just end up with a bunch of half-baked ideas that never get off the ground.

Or you go after an idea because you're not really confident yet and someone else said this is the right way to do it. At the end of the day, you realize it's not the right way for you.

Can you relate to that? I know I have definitely been there. It is time to stop should-ing all over yourself. There is always going to be noise pulling you in a million directions. There are always going to be people telling you that their way is the best way.

There is Only ONE Right Way - Yours!

The only thing that you need to worry about is finding your way, the way that will work best for you, your business, and your lifestyle.

In fact, I had an amazing full day VIP session with one of my private clients where we settled in for 2 days to map out the business she was creating.

One of her biggest struggles was that she had invested a ton of time, energy and money for all of these high level coaching and training programs, and everyone was telling her what she should be doing in her business in a way that in her gut, in her heart, just didn't feel like her.

It wasn't who she was, how she operated and it didn't align with who she wanted to be in the world... but she also felt trapped because she had paid so much to these experts.

The first step is to really understand what is behind your desire to be an entrepreneur.

What is Your Why?

This might sound like a huge, huge question, but you have to have a real strong reason for why you're in business. What is driving you forward? What is the reason that you are getting up and working on this thing during the good times and the bad every single day?

There are a lot of reasons why people get into business and I think being really clear and honest with yourself about what motivates you is the first step to making sure that everything starts to fall into alignment.

Here's a few that I hear a lot::

Is your Why to do meaningful work? Is this the work that you feel you were called to do? This is your dharma; it's your calling. Maybe it's just something that you really get a lot of fulfillment out of. You might not consider it a "calling" per se, but it feels like the most fulfilling work for you; more fulfilling than any other type of work that you've done or that you could do right now.

Is your big Why that you want to be a lifestyle entrepreneur? You want to live a specific lifestyle that you think being an entrepreneur will provide. You're hoping that it will give you freedom, it will give you the income that you need to pay your bills with ease and do everything in your life that you really want to do.

Maybe your big Why is that you want to use your business as a platform to share a message with the world. You have something to say and you want to get it into the hands and the hearts of as many people as possible.

Or, maybe your Why is to use your business as a vehicle that allows you to give back in a really epic way. This could be a social giving component like Toms Shoes or maybe you want to be a philanthropist and you know that you can help more people if you personally have a higher income.

Ultimately, finding your Why is essential to making sure that your business is in alignment with you, with what you value, with what matters most to you.

Your Why helps you facilitate this whole decision-making process by helping you figure out what you need to say "no" to in order to make room for the business and life that you really want.

Begin With The End in Mind

This is how we align our business with our values and with what matters to us. That's what allows us to get really clear about what it is that we're trying to create. What is it actually going to look like? How would we describe it in very real, visceral terms?

I love this strategy that takes us a level deeper from Cameron Herold's book *Double Double*. It's a little bit more geared towards a traditional or startup world. But, I've found an amazing amount of value from this book. The biggest part of it came from this exercise that he calls The Painted Picture.

If you've ever done a vision board, you've started this process. You've started envisioning what it is that you wanted to have or experience. This takes it a level deeper.

A painted picture is describing in detail what your business and lifestyle will look like in the future. You can actually tell somebody, "*This is what I want my day to look like. These are the activities I want to be doing. This is the type of programs and services and offerings I want to have in my business. These are the people I want to work with. This is how it's all going to really look,*" in so much detail that it's as if you were writing the script for the film of your dream day in your life and business.

I want to drive this piece home because I think it's so important: *you have to include your life in the painted picture*. Because if you don't, you'll basically crowd it out with business. You will fill your painted picture with what your business is going to look like and you end up overestimating what we can accomplish in our business at the expense of our life.

When you have your painted picture, you have clear focus and direction.

You know exactly what kind of business you are working towards. And most importantly, it will help you to say no to anything that veers off course or that can become a distraction.

Your Painted Picture is extremely helpful because entrepreneurs are idea machines. We can come up with ideas nonstop, all day long... but most of those ideas are distractions. They're shiny objects. They're not necessarily going to take us where we want to go or help us feel like we're doing the work that we need to do in the world.

Your biggest challenge as an entrepreneur will be learning to say NO so you can stay focused and connected to your Why. Your Why is that north star; it's where we're pointing our compass, where we're putting our strategy map in place so that we can step by step have this clear point on the horizon that we are working towards.

If you don't have a painted picture and you don't know what you're creating, it's really hard to figure out what steps you need to take next.

Then, you'll find yourself taking actions here and there, but there's no forward momentum. You're kind of dancing all over the place. And, while the dancing could be fun -- don't get me wrong; the journey is just as important as the destination -- it can't just be about the journey.

You have to move forward and make that forward momentum if you want to have a profitable and sustainable business that will create this lifestyle that you really want. We're going to start talking about how we can bring all of this together inside of your painted picture.

Your Painted Picture

Let's start looking at how we can begin creating a painted picture for a year from now. Imagine you're leaning out into the future. You're going to do a little bit of daydreaming. Imagine that you're playing a movie in your head about what your life and your business would be like a year from today. This is your ideal perfect day, maybe your idea business a year from now.

Again, I'll reiterate: it's only a year that we're focused on. As you build and grow your business, you can lengthen the timeline - but a year is super tangible and much easier for your first strategic planning exercise.

A year from today, you're just dreaming through and thinking of what your business and life is going to look like. Probably the easiest way to get started is to think about where your business and life going to change.

What would you like to do differently? Understanding the contrast between where you are now and where you want to be will help you figure out how far apart you are so that you can start moving forward.

What do you want to be creating in your business? It could be new content, this could be creating a new book, writing a program, anything creative-focused.

What do you want to give? Do you have a desire to give back in some way? Whether it's giving something to a community that is supporting you in your business, or does it mean giving something back to your family? Does it mean giving to a nonprofit that you really care about?

What do you want to do? For your business, this could be: Do I want to be working one-on-one with people or do I want to be focused on working in groups? In your life, it could be, "I want to be running more or I want to be having family game nights more." What is it that you want to be doing every day or every week in your life and in your business?

What do you want to have a year from now? This is actually about having something, so this is maybe what most of us have done in the past whenever we've created a vision board or a dream board. We usually cut out pictures of the things we want. There's a place for that.

I think there are definitely areas of your life that people like to upgrade. Maybe you want a nicer computer, maybe you want to commit to shopping for only the highest quality food possible. Whatever it is, it's okay to want what you want and upgrade your life.

What does this life feel like to you? I think it's important, again, to look at what you need to change from today. A big part of this, for me, as I've done this practice year after year has been moving from what felt like a very, very busy, almost rat race type of life where I was always caught up in something, to feeling like I had a lot of spaciousness and breathing room. I want to maintain this feeling about my life.

What do you want to be experiencing? Experiencing is what actually you are doing all day long. What are the things that you want to do with your family? What experiences do you want to have in your business? Do you want to have the experience of saying you are a published author? Do you want to have the experience of saying you are a speaker and you've spoken on the stage? Do you want to have an experience taking your children on an amazing road trip across the country?

Day 11:: Fired Up & Focused Challenge!

Okay, time to get into inspired action. Spend some time dreaming on those prompts::

Think about your Why.

What is driving you? Why did you start this business? What's really important for you?

It's okay for you to say that your why is to create a lifestyle for yourself and your family. It's okay for you to say your why is to make a lot of money so that you can give it all away. Your why is yours. You don't have to share it with anybody. It's something only you need to know.

Don't base your Why on someone else's, and don't try to compare. Just discern what it is that's most important to you and put it somewhere where you can see it on a regular basis, so you can stay motivated and engaged even when you're facing challenges.

Create your painted picture.

Actually write it out. Write out what you want to be doing, being, having, feeling, experiencing, and creating in your business, your life.

You can also talk about your health and your well-being, your wellness. You can talk about your spirituality or your religion. You can talk about your family or your relationships. You can also include fun -- things that you just want to experience because you don't think a bucket list is something we should put off until we're at the end of our life; we should be checking it off right now.

Day 12:: The Problem with Goal Setting

The previous chapter guided you through this amazing exercise to paint a picture of the life and the business that you want to have a year from now. And today, I want you to start living into that vision.

To be sure you're ready to make that vision your reality, I want to talk about something that, unfortunately, throws some people off course. It's the reason I gave up goal-setting.

This might surprise you. You might have expected me to dive into how we can set goals the correct, SMART way in order to reach your vision. If you've gotten to know me by now, you know that I naturally wired as a goal-setting, goal-getting, type-A, overachiever workaholic.

I have always been the type of person who, when I had something that I wanted, it was never a matter of if I would achieve it, it was just a matter of when.

I could get focused. I could be disciplined. I could work my fingers to the bone until I got what I wanted. Then I hit burnout. I started experiencing panic attacks. I had debilitating anxiety.

That's when I realized that maybe this whole goal-setting approach that I learned from my MBA program, success coaches, and the whole personal development space, maybe it was actually hurting me. Maybe there were some problems with the way we were approaching goal-setting.

The Journey is Important

The problem with goal setting is that it leads us to believe that we have to put the destination above the journey. We have to throw ourselves at something way more than we need to in order to get where we want to go.

This is why you will see so many people, especially at New Year's setting these resolutions to lose weight and get healthy. They throw themselves at it 150%. They go on the crash diet, they hit the gym hard every day until the day comes where they have a bite of a cookie or they start to have such soreness that they can't get to the gym one day for a workout.

It is only a matter of them falling completely off the wagon and the next year they're probably setting the same resolution again. It's this vicious, vicious cycle that we put ourselves in. We feel like we have to be all or nothing.

The problem with goal-setting is you can't control that outcome. It would be like you saying as an entrepreneur that your big goal is to reach six figures. I think that is a great goal. Usually, for many of us it represents having a comfortable lifestyle and a profitable and sustainable business.

But the challenge here is there is no easy button to push and suddenly $100,000 appears. Sure, there are a lot of things you can do to influence your income and track revenue. But, at the end of the day, you still can't guarantee that you'll make $100,000.

Same thing with another popular metric: how big your community grows. I hear so many people say I want to have 10,000 people on my email list. Ten thousand people is the magic number where suddenly you can have this profitable, sustainable coaching and teaching business.

Well, the problem again is you can say that you want to get that goal, but you can't control it. There's no button. You have influence, you have tools to climb toward it, but no guarantee that you'll reach the top.

Rituals + Systems + Action = Results

What happens if you can't control the outcome? You have to realize that the outcomes are the byproducts of the rituals, the systems and the action steps that you take every single day.

The outcomes are what you would like to achieve, but if you've spent all your time focused on them you tend to get on this all or nothing mindset that can really be detrimental to you. It's not about working harder. It's not about knuckling down, grinning and bearing it, working at this goal at the risk of giving up your life, your health, your well-being, your family, your friends.

One of the problems I see with goal-setting is it creates this vicious cycle of achieving. It leaves us feeling like we will be happy when we achieve that goal. Then we get there and we just look for the next thing to achieve.

Research is showing us that this yo-yo effect, where we are going back and forth from working insanely hard towards a goal then either hitting burnout and freezing up, or becoming addicted to the achievement, is putting too much pressure on us.

Consistent Progress Leads to Results

What is the desired outcome that you want to live into?

This is something from your painted picture; something from your business and your life. What do you want to be doing, having, feeling, experiencing in your painted picture one year from today?

What action steps do you need to take in order to move closer day by day by day?

Which system will help you be consistent?

I have found this to be the secret sauce. This is the key. If you have a system in place it will help you stay on track and if you have a ritual that it ensures that you are supporting yourself, that you are taking precious care of yourself, that you are taking care of your personal needs, your physical needs, your health and happiness needs, you are providing yourself with the right environment and the right mindset that you need in order to sit down and consistently be ready to get to work.

Let's say that your goal, your desired outcome for the end of this year is to have built your community to 1,000 people on your email list. This is a great goal for someone who is pretty new to starting their business.

What would be the first action step that you need to take that would start to move you towards that goal? Again, it will influence whether or not you're getting close.

A great one, a great action step would be to be submitting two guest posts per month. This puts you in front of new audiences. It gets new eyeballs learning about you, about what you are about, what you are interested in, what you are an expert on. And, if you do it correctly, it will draw those people back to your business, to your website and your email list.

What is the system that will help you to be able to create, pitch and post on two sites per month?

The system is the weekly writing schedule. This is where you've actually made time for this to happen on your model calendar. You've got a block of time each and every week where you're sitting down and making it happen. Without that system, then you tend to get out of alignment with working towards your goals.

One of the rituals that you can do to help ensure that you're staying on the system is having these work rituals that we've been talking about so far in the challenge. This could be setting the stage, those pre work rituals. They get you emotionally and energetically in the right space.

This is where you are not multitasking, you're single tasking. You're doing a few rounds of Pomodoros during that weekly block of time that you've set aside just to write guests posts.

You'll start to see how, even if you only have a one or two hour block of time to focus on this specific goal, by the end of every week, every month, every quarter, end of the year, you'll be dramatically closer to that desired outcome than if you were to try to wing it.

Day 12:: Fired Up & Focused Challenge!

What do you need to do consistently to live into your painted picture? I want you to brainstorm three key action steps that you can do in order to get where you want to go one year from today.

1)

2)

3)

What systems do you need to implement in order to make consistent progress? Does it mean that you need to plug it into your calendar? Does it mean that you need to make it a point to get out there and meet new people? Does it mean that you need to ask for referrals or upgrade a skill set and make sure you are making time to learn how to do this thing?

What rituals will support your efforts? What will help you to operate at your highest level that allows you to take amazing care of yourself? That ensures you are not working harder, you are working smarter. That allows you to create more ease and spaciousness as you start working towards this big vision you've created for yourself.

Day 13:: Money Flows
Where Your Attention Goes

If you are really being the CEO of your life and your business, what would your relationship to money look like?

Would you stuff all of your bills in a drawer - not even opening the envelopes to check on the balances?

Would you put off your bookkeeping until the very last minute and then race around trying to find all those receipts and documents you need to so that you can pay your taxes on time?

Would you forget about unpaid invoices and following up with people when their payments don't come through?

No? Well, most of us know that if we're going to be the CEOs of our life and our business, a big piece of that job description is learning to manage the money; making sure that everything is flowing to us so we can keep the {virtual} doors open.

Remember, energy flows where attention goes. When you pay attention to something, more energy will be sent there. Replace the world energy with the word money: Money flows where attention goes.

The truth is, at its very essence, money is what we use to represent the energetic exchange between our clients and us.

When we're offering ourselves, our services, our knowledge, or our time, we need to be compensated so we're having an equal, energetic exchange between us and our clients. If we are undercharging or not getting paid, then we're not balanced; neither side is coming into the agreement honoring each other's time and efforts.

When you feel like you are honoring yourself, when you're getting paid your worth, you start to heal any wounds that you have around money and you begin to manifest more money simply because you start to appreciate it, pay attention to it, and have a more positive relationship to it.

Today - I don't want to overwhelm you with things that include spreadsheets or calculations or budgets or spending plans. I don't want you to feel guilt or overwhelm or shame around money.

We're focused instead on creating a huge emotional, energetic shift so that you can feel happy and grateful for the money that is flowing to you. In my experience, the happier and more grateful you are about what's coming to you, the more of that you will attract into your life and business.

To get started, download and print out the workbook that goes along with this book at http://www.firedupandfocused.com/book. You'll be using the Money Clarity worksheet.

Print out the worksheet because it's something you want to look at every single day. In fact, I keep mine in my desk where I can pull it out - I have a little writing surface in my old fashioned teacher's desk that slides right below the main desktop. I pull it out and update how much money flows to me every single day. It's made such a huge difference in my money mindset.

Write down your desired revenue for this month.

If you're not sure what your desired revenue is, you might want to spend a little bit of time thinking about this. What do you need in order to run your business and pay yourself? Once you have those baseline numbers, you might want to add an additional 30% on top of that. That should usually cover any taxes or unexpected expenses.

Once you have that desired income goal, then you'll be able to start seeing if you're on track. You may have a higher desired revenue based on where you are in your business, but don't go crazy with setting a really out there desired revenue goal right now.

Make sure that it's within reach. If you've only been making a couple thousand dollars every month, writing in something like $20,000 is going to make you feel really defeated. Keep it within a reasonable range; something that maybe just stretches you a little bit or makes you feel a little bit nervous and excited, but nothing that feels like you couldn't achieve it.

The goal here is to start paying attention to the money flowing to you and allow it to grow as you pay attention to your money, not to push yourself so far out of your comfort zone that your monkey mind just whips around and pulls you right back into making less and feeling shameful or afraid of money.

Write down all the incoming revenue so far this month.

Once you have that desired revenue goal for this month, I want you to write down everything you've been paid every day so far this month. You're literally tracking when money is showing up for you. If you got paid $500 on the 15th of the month, you write in $500.

Only write down money that actually hits your account, not when someone says, "I want to join you for this!" or, "I want to work with you," but they haven't handed you a check, they haven't paid for the thing. Make sure you're only writing this down when money is actually in your possession.

Write down all found, freebie, and bonus money.

There is another column there that I want you to pay attention to. This is all about found, freebie and bonus money. The point of this is to show you that you are abundant. You have prosperity flowing to you.

When your grandmother sends you a birthday card and it has $50 in it. When you put on your winter coat and realize there's a $20 bill in the pocket. You go out to coffee with a friend and she picked up the tab. You write that extra $5 in there because that is found money that you didn't expect, but it still adds up over the month, over the year.

Finally, express gratitude.

Every single time you write something in on one of these columns throughout the month -- whether it's somebody who paid you or somebody who paid for your coffee - just simply put your hand over your heart and say,

"Thank you. Thank you for the abundance in my life. Thank you for these amazing clients who believe in the work that I'm doing. Thank you for my friend who gave me this lovely gift. Thank you, thank you, thank you."

The more that you express your gratitude; the more you shift your energy around money. The more you shift your energy around money, the more you shift your emotions around money. Then, you'll start to shift your story around money. Suddenly, you start to attract more of what you're grateful for.

I know this seems so incredibly simple, but the truth is that diving into the deep end of all the financial stuff, of serious accounting and bookkeeping and high level financial planning, it can backfire on us, bringing up feelings of shame and guilt and not enough-ness.

Don't focus on that right now. We can dive into those piece by piece in more manageable chunks once we found a part of it that we can latch onto with positivity, with gratefulness and feel empowered. This small step leads to taking the next small step and the next small step until, suddenly, you really feel like the CEO of your life and your business.

Day 13:: Fired Up & Focused Challenge!

Get into inspired action!

- Make sure you download the worksheet.
- Write in your desired revenue for this month.
- Each time you get paid, write it down.
- Each time you have found money or bonus money or free money, write it down.
- Each time you write something on this money clarity worksheet, feel gratitude for the abundance in your life.

Day 14:: Breaking Through Your Upper Limits

Have you ever experienced this::

Things are finally taking off for you in your business... and then you get sick. Not just a few sniffles sick but days in bed feeling like HELL sick.

Or maybe you come home to pick a fight with your partner.

Or you find yourself worrying that it's not gonna last, that it's all gonna go away, or maybe even that you don't think you're worthy of your new success.

Sound familiar?

Turns out, each one of us carries around this unconscious idea of how much happiness, success, joy or love we can have. And when you start pushing against this unconscious limit, your monkey mind starts to pull you back or look for ways to self-sabotage and keep you in your comfort zone.

Gay Hendricks, author of *The Big Leap*, says that each of us has an inner thermostat setting that determines how much love, success and creativity we allow ourselves to enjoy. That thermostat setting usually gets programmed in early childhood. And, once programmed, our Upper Limit thermostat setting holds us back from enjoying all the love, financial abundance and creativity that's rightfully ours.

Gay says that when we start hitting that threshold we start to mess up other areas of our life because we don't feel worthy, we feel like success will result in abandonment, we feel that shining brightly is a crime and that success brings more burdens.

And we ALL experience upper limits... myself included! As soon as I hit another growth spurt, I find myself feeling overwhelmed, on edge, and hearing the same negative thoughts whirring through my head.

Upper Limits. They know exactly how to push your buttons.

Now that I know what to look for - I know that for me, there are lots of tools to help me get out of my own way::

- **Intensive self-care.** Lots of great healthy food. Massage. Sleep and more sleep. EFT {aka Tapping}.

- **More down time.** For me - this usually means a *Downton Abbey* binge. While cozy in bed with hot tea.

- **Crossing things OFF the to-do-list.** Simplifying. Getting extra help {thank you thank you to my amazing team!}.

- **Spending more time moving my body**. Getting on my mat. Going for a long walk.

- **Allowing myself to just have silly fun!** Painting with my kids. Swinging on the swing set.

The truth is - Upper Limits are a part of the entrepreneurial + personal development journey. Each time you begin to break through in an area of your life and business, you'll likely find yourself fighting the same Upper Limit monsters.

I'm sharing this because Fired Up + Focused is a catalyst for explosive growth. Each of these small steps add up to huge transformation in your business. At this stage, you may start experiencing these upper limits and feel frustrated by your business.

Once you know what's happening, you can turn things around and begin the process of expanding how much happiness or success you're ready to feel - here's some of my favorite ideas::

- Take amazing care of yourself.

- Clean up your money habits.

- Start a gratitude practice.

- De-clutter and beautify your space.

- Do a random act of kindness.

Be aware of any Upper Limit problems - especially when loads of good stuff starts to come your way! Pay special attention to your thoughts, behaviors, and actions when you start living into your dream.

Ask yourself "*How much success, happiness, joy, and love am I really wanting to experience?*"... and if the answer is "*ALL I CAN!*", then know that you can live in alignment with that dream when you face your upper limits.

You rock for bringing everything you've got to this challenge. It takes so much courage and faith to follow your passion and your dreams. It's NOT the easy road - goodness knows it would be much easier to clock in each day for a J.O.B.!

But when you choose YOURSELF - when you fully commit to making a difference in the world through work that completely lights you up - something amazing happens. You give those around you hope... and permission to follow their passions.

Today is your day for integration + implementation. It's the perfect time to catch up or review previous challenges, take some time to reflect, and celebrate your progress!

Day 15:: The Difference Between a Hobby and a Business

The role of a CEO is all about the big picture. This is where so many of us get excited about our businesses… we absolutely adore dreaming up big, innovative ideas!

While there is a lot of talk about $10,000 - $100,000 - $1,000,000 ideas, the truth is ideas without inspired action are $0. It's up to you to implement and see those ideas become reality.

So how do you choose which ideas to pursue? Which idea will finally help your business take off? How can you make that transition from a side-hustle into full-time entrepreneurship?

Over the last five or so years, I've developed a framework to help solopreneurs sort through all the big ideas to find their unique Business Sweet Spot. By understanding this concept, you'll have a powerful new way to quickly filter through all those big ideas and focus in on what will make the biggest impact for you and your business.

First, let's start with what influenced the creation of the Business Sweet Spot - because the truth is, I just didn't dream it up one day completely on my own!

The Hedgehog Concept

The Business Sweet Spot evolved from the work of Jim Collins in his book *From Good to Great*. Jim did an amazing amount of research into some of the biggest and most successful corporations in the world to figure out what it was that made them so successful - head and shoulders above their competitors - even when they were selling the same types of products to the same types of audience for about the same price point.

What was it that these companies understood that made them so much more successful? As he researched, he realized that all these companies had three key elements that together made them dominate their market. He called this the Hedgehog Concept. There are three parts of original The Hedgehog Concept::

Part 1:: Passion. Companies that really thrived had a very specific vision that kept their business focused in a clear direction. This trickled down through the companies as part of their culture - everyone was working towards a common goal.

Part 2:: Best in World. Companies that were the top of their market were at the top for a reason - they stayed 100% focused on what they could do better than anyone. Anything outside this core competency was a distraction and not pursued.

Part 3:: Economic Engine. Companies that weren't just good - but great - understood exactly what drove their revenues. Remember the 80/20 rule? These great companies knew that 80% of their revenues came from only 20% of their products or services... so they spent most of their focus optimizing and growing that 20%.

This concept makes so much sense for bigger corporations; translating it into something that was useful for solopreneurs takes a little more finessing.

Many entrepreneurs I serve struggle not with having passion but having many passions! These multipassionate entrepreneurs often struggle to find focus because they feel like they are choosing one passion over another.

Most of us naturally gravitate towards businesses that are aligned with our strengths. But being the best in the world? That's a lot of pressure for a health coach or creative who knows there are thousands of talented people just like them doing similar work. If you're not sure you're the best, how can you stand out?

And understanding what fuels their economic engine is easier said than done when you're just in the startup phase or first few years of your business.

The Business Sweet Spot

After working with hundreds of my own clients, I started to tweak the Hedgehog to fit the needs of a lifestyle entrepreneur - someone who is a solopreneur or running a small team. The Business Sweet Spot helps you to get instant clarity so you stay focused on your goals, make better decisions for your business, and avoid distractions.

Passion Fuels You

Like the Hedgehog, passion fuels entrepreneurs! It's really the defining characteristic when you think about heart-centered entrepreneurs. In fact, this is why many of us became heart-centered entrepreneurs to begin with because we pursued an interest or a hobby that we couldn't stop obsessing over.

The difference between a hobby and a business? You've gotta make sure that passion is something deeper than a passing phase. Business success comes from having a deeper level of passion, a bigger truth that you want to share with the world.

This is where it can start to get deep. We are talking about something that you feel so strongly about that you just want to shout it from the rooftops.

Here is the thing though: **Passion alone isn't enough**.

Think about it this way. How many raving sports fans do you know? How many times did their team win just because of the passionate cheering? That's just not how it works. There is more to it than that.

Let's take a look at these other two areas that we have to bring into the picture in order to find our business sweet spot.

Purpose Differentiates You

This is your unique expression of divine gifts that only you have to share with the world. It's a combination of strengths, talents, life experience, education, and skills that you bring to your work.

This is really important because so many people only consider their strengths. They don't think about their life experience, education, or how their life's journey is flavoring the way they approach their work and how they do what they do.

All of that plays a part. It really is this magical, secret sauce of what you've been working on your entire life.

One of the most important parts of your divine gifts? They come effortlessly to you. Where others have to work really, really hard to get better at these strengths, these divine gifts, you can just work on them a little bit and grow exponentially.

If you've ever watched somebody who is a musical prodigy, they can sit down without having practiced for weeks and they still are at the top of their game… whereas everyone else has to practice six hours a day just to keep up with them.

That is speaking from experience. I've been there.

I was a French horn major in college. I practiced 20 hours per week on top of all my ensemble classes and still found myself hustling to keep up with an amazingly talented player who rarely practiced. It was so frustrating… especially if you, like me, had been told that hard work is more important than talent.

Turns out, the magic comes when you combine hard work plus talent.

When you really step into your purpose, you begin to work in your zone of genius. Suddenly, you have a trump card you can play to differentiate yourself from so many others who do similar work.

Now, we understand why passion is so essential, it's that bigger why, the deeper truth that you have to share with the world. We also understand why your purpose, the unique way that you approach your work, your zone of genius is the key ingredient to differentiate you from the hundreds or thousands of other people doing similar work.

Finally, the economic engine, the profits, how do you actually make money?

But here is the key: If you only focus on profits, you actually will struggle more. I find that it is more essential, the real secret to entrepreneurial success, lies in understanding your perfect for you clients. The final ingredient to unlocking your Business Sweet Spot? It's your peeps.

People Pay You

This is the biggest difference between an expensive hobby and a booming business. Unlocking your profit starts with understanding your people.

This is opposite of what a lot of heart-centered entrepreneurs focus on. Many are so caught up in their passion and what they want to be sharing that they start creating in a vacuum. When you begin creating in insolation, it's extremely disappointing when you realize that people don't actually want the thing you've created!

Without people to serve, there is no business. That's the number one way to ensure you have a profitable business? Listen, listen, and listen to those you want to serve. When you're tapped into the needs and desires of your dream clients, you can much more easily create programs, products, and services that are exactly what they are looking for.

If you've fallen into the trap of believing that your work speaks for itself or that they are instantly going to get why they need your thing, then you will struggle to turn those people into paying customers.

You're peeps have to see the value of what you have to offer. They have to understand why it is relevant to them and that you created it to help them solve their problem or fulfill a desire.

Mindful Marketing is the Language of Your Dream Clients

It's all about connecting those dots and truly communicating the value of what you have to offer. When you can speak their language, you can help your dream clients realize that what you have created is exactly what will help them get from Point A to Point B.

Suddenly, you don't have to sell yourself so hard. Instead, they are sitting there reading the information you've put in front of them, nodding their head saying, *"Yes, this is what I have been looking for. This will help me get where I want to go."*

Sounds good, right? We want to make it easy for people to understand why we've created what we have created and that it is here to help them.

Case Study:: Racheal's Business Sweet Spot

Now I want to share with you, as a working example, my own business sweet spot. As I've been working and playing with this methodology over the past eight or so years, this has evolved, it's gotten deeper and richer and more nuanced.

As I peel back the curtain, know that this is not perfect. It's a work in progress. It's always evolving. I'm always understanding and learning more about how I can best serve. As you begin to work with people and get more experience in your business, you'll find these deeper, more nuanced layers that are what creates your signature, trademark style in how you are approaching your work.

When I started my first business, The Yogipreneur in 2008, I initially thought that my passion in my business was bringing together two loves:: yoga and business strategy. It was a great starting point that helped me to define my niche and my direction.

After several years of running this business, my message started to evolve from just yoga-specific business advice. I started bringing my yogi mindset through to talk about inspiring more ease into other areas of business and lifestyle design.

As I launched my second business under my own personal brand in 2014, I built my entire message around this passion for inspiring more ease and less stress in your business and life. From the free Fired Up & Focused Challenge to my paid offerings Conscious Business Design and Sweet Spot Online Mastermind, inspiring ease is the theme that weaves throughout my body of work.

The next area of My Business Sweet Spot is my purpose. When I first started looking at my strengths, the "*What can I be the best in the world at,*" that part of the original Hedgehog Concept, I initially looked at things like my strengths finder and all of these different assessments I had taken.

I thought my strengths were all about my classical business training through getting an MBA, my experience working with big multi-million dollar corporations, and my natural ability go through tons of information and synthesize it all to lay out an action plan. It's why I've naturally done well as a strategist - this is in my DNA!

But I'm not unique in this! There are thousands of business coaches. There are so many people who are great at mapping out a strategy. What made me unique and different in this work?

I discovered that it was all about un-complicating business strategy and making it applicable to lifestyle entrepreneurs.

I hear this over and over again from my students who've worked with business coaches. They are always saying to me, *"You made this so easy for me to understand. You were able to break it down in a way that I could actually take action on. I didn't feel stupid or like I couldn't actually do what you taught."*

It's easy to create something complicated. What's not easy? Making it simple so that anyone can understand and implement it. That's my divine gift.

The final piece of my Business Sweet Spot is knowing who I'm here to serve. When I launched my first business, I was sure that my people were yoga studio owners and yoga entrepreneurs who were struggling to grow their business - so it made sense that I started by focusing on 1x1 consulting for yoga businesses.

But there was an interesting challenge - the people I wanted to serve often couldn't afford to hire a consultant like myself to come in and work closely with their business.

It was an interesting challenge to face - my dream clients needed more than just a book and they hated being one of thousands in a big class. They wanted a more intimate environment to get support and training without the price tag of hiring a 1x1 consultant. I took the next step towards serving more people {and in turn, generating more profits} when I created my first online coaching program Conscious Business Design.

As I started focusing more of my attention online vs. in person, my message of more ease and less stress started to attract even more types of entrepreneurs. Health coaches, tarot card readers, bloggers, designers, photographers, wedding planners, life coaches, doulas… I realized my message was reaching a much bigger audience than yogis alone. That's when I decided to launch RachealCook.com, created the Fired Up & Focused Challenge, and started talking to lifestyle entrepreneurs like myself who wanted to make a life and a living, doing what they love.

Day 15:: Fired Up & Focused Challenge!

Now that we have taken a look at the Sweet Spot, I encourage you to get into inspired action. Grab the Sweet Spot Guide when you register for your book bonus bundle at http://www.firedupandfocused.com/book. It's a beautifully compiled guide full of questions that will help you to unlock each of these three areas.

Answer each of the questions. You can take some time to develop your answers here, but even if all you do right now is just jot down some quick notes, it's going to trigger something in you. It will start to unlock things that you might not have thought about before.

The questions are the real deal. I've heard so many people say, "*This was the first time I really understood who my ideal clients are and how I can uniquely serve them.*"

What are 3 ways you can integrate your Business Sweet Spot into your existing business and marketing?

Day 16:: Uncomplicate Your Business

Moving on from the big picture, 10,000x view of what you're creating in your business, it's time to get laser-focused. I know that after discovering these exciting things like your business sweet spot and your painted picture, you're probably swimming with ideas of how you can move your business forward.

As an entrepreneur, you're probably an idea machine. We love coming up with new ideas, new ways that we can serve, new ways that we can get our message out into the world and that we can grow our business.

The problem with this is sometimes it can be a little overwhelming. As Richard Branson says, *"Ideas are like buses. There is always another one coming."*

When there's always this onslaught of ideas happening for us creative types, how do you know which idea is the right idea to act on first?

I've got a very simple and strategic framework to help you to start to vet your ideas. I have to do this to filter through the lists of ideas that I'm always coming up with. Yes, I said lists, plural. That's because I'm just like you, I've always got new ideas bubbling up and I keep them on a running document that I call my Idea Parking Lot.

An Idea Parking Lot is really simple. It can be a journal, a Google Doc, an Evernote. The key is to create one area where you'll keep all those great ideas so you can come back to them later instead of changing directions every other week with these shiny new ideas.

Every once in a while I will check in, review it, and see which idea I might want to pull out and start working on. Some of them sit there for a long time. I know that I've got to be very strategic about which ideas I take action on because like we've discussed throughout Fired Up and Focused, I have to make sure that I am both moving my business forward while also taking precious care of myself and my family; having plenty of time and space for balance in my life.

3 Criteria for Your Next Big Idea

Without a decision making process, it's really easy to get caught up in a bright and shiny idea that turns out to be a distraction from what you really need to be focused on in your business.

1:: Most Profitable Idea

Which idea is the most profitable?

Now there are two answers you must consider for this question::

1. Do you need cash flow ASAP?

Bills are coming due, you've got to pay the rent and you know that you need to be turning something around and making money within the next 30 days, then chances are *your most profitable idea is going to be exchanging your time for money by working with someone one-on-one as a teacher, coach or service provider.*

Now you may be saying, "*Wait, I wanted to move away from that dollars for hours model. I wanted to create something that was leveraged or passive and allowed me to work with more people for less time."*

I hear you.

This is what I spend all my time inside Conscience Business Design helping people learn and implement in their businesses. But here is the truth that most people just aren't telling you - It takes time to create that model and it is hard to create leveraged or passive income streams when you are strapped for cash and feeling financial pressure.

The moment that you release that pressure simply by bringing in a few private teaching, coaching or service clients, suddenly you have the financial cushion that you need. You have some runway where you can start to work towards those leveraged or passive income streams without putting unnecessary stress on yourself.

2. Do you have a steady income stream that covers the bases?

Maybe you're building your business on the side while your full-time gig pays the bills. Maybe you've got some existing retainer clients that cover the expenses. The key here is that you have either existing income or a big financial cushion. If yes, then you can start to think about the longer term profitable ideas.

The truth is the leveraged and passive income streams {working in groups, creating online programs, and creating a completely automated, virtual product} have more capacity for long-term profitability.

But I see a lot of people rushing into those too fast without a safety net. These types of offerings often take a lot longer than you think to get off the ground. It takes a lot of work and a lot of moving parts to create leveraged or passive income. In fact, I'd say that it took at least 200 hours to create my first multi-media online program.

You'll also find that this model requires much more marketing because you'll need a bigger audience. You have to get eyeballs on it in order to make it work.

On the flip side, focusing your attention on 1x1 work doesn't require nearly as many clients to be profitable and you can often fill those spots by asking for referrals and offering the opportunity to your existing community.

I just wanted to throw those two little caveats there so you have a realistic picture of what's going to be the most profitable idea for you to pursue based on your current financial situation and the timeframe that you really have.

2:: Most Sustainable Idea

What is the most sustainable idea?

What idea can you commit to for 90 days, and will you still be able to ensure that your needs are met? Be honest with yourself. How long of a timeframe can you really do that hustling without feeling burned out?

I know that personally, I really can only go for a few weeks at a time at that pace. Otherwise, I start to feel a little worn out. I start to notice that my voice starts to go away and I need a lot more self-care, so I have to make sure that I am planning accordingly.

This is really important because we've talked so much about creating balance in your life. Know that balance is not a noun. It is not something you achieve and you have it like a trophy on the shelf. It's a verb. It is something you are actively working on.

You have to make sure that in the act of balancing over the course of a week or month or season, you have taken care of yourself. You've invested time and energy into your own self-care, into connecting and being with your family and your friends, getting eight hours of sleep at night, making sure that you have time for fitness and get all of these different pieces that we require for a rich, vibrant life.

Is this project going to require you to dramatically shift your schedule for an extended period of time?

It might! You have to really decide if that is okay or not for you. Personally, I know that about 80% of the year my schedule is really laid back; it's exactly how I like it. I am running Conscience Business Design, I am working with very few private clients, and it really allows me to make sure everyone's needs are met in a way that is sustainable.

The other 20%? It's a hustle. I wish I could say you would never have to hustle again, but the truth is, if you are launching something, if you are running a challenge or opening the doors to a new program or building a lot of buzz about something that you are doing, it will require you to up your time commitment for that short period.

A big element of building a business that loves me back is making sure that after those busy hustle periods, I'm able to take some time off to decompress. Building in those business savasanas immediately after running the live Fired Up & Focused Challenge or launching Conscious Business Design helps me to bring back that balance more quickly {and avoid burnout}.

Know yourself and know how much time you need in order to rebound from those busy times.

3:: Most Awesome Idea

What is the most awesome idea?

Of course, awesome is totally subjective. This is all about what's lighting you up the most. What are you completely excited about?

Ultimately, the ideas on the list that you're feeling the least excitement about are not going to share your best work. You're going to lose steam and come up with reasons why you don't want to do it. Then, at the end of the day, you're going to feel like you made zero progress.

It can't just be about the money. It has to be about what your soul is calling you to do and to put out to the world.

The 90 Day Plan

Now that you've vetted some ideas, hopefully you're down to one, the one that you are going to commit to for the next 90 days. This is such a perfect time frame because it's just long enough to make meaningful progress towards a big goal but not so long that you lose the enthusiasm.

That doesn't mean that it is all hustle for the entire 90 days, but it does mean that you have a clear end date in mind for when you are going to launch this thing or when you are going to get to a major milestone. You might not be able to create and launch something new in 90 days. You might just be able to create it or just be able to do the marketing plan for it. That's totally okay.

You have to decide though what the major goal is for this big idea and then map out your action plan to help you reach that goal.

Let's take a look at this and reverse engineer this plan so that you can actually put the pieces in your calendar, in your project management system, and move forward with this big idea.

Reverse engineering means starting with the end milestone and planning backwards. Here's the example we are going to work with so I can show you how you can reverse engineer your action plan.

Let's say our end milestone is having five new private clients. You're offering some sort of service where you work with someone one-on-one like a designer, copywriter, et cetera. Lots of us work with people in some sort of one-on-one capacity.

Simply by saying what you want that end result to be, that big milestone at the end of the 90 days, then you can start to work backwards and figure out what action steps need to happen in order to get you to that end result.

This is totally telling the universe, *"Hey, this is what I want to have happen. I want to welcome five new private clients."*

Let's move backwards from those five new private clients. Before they sign on that dotted line with you and pay you, you have to formally invite them to work with you, which means you have to have an agreement and an invoice ready to go. Those are two pieces of the puzzle that you'll want to have ready so that you can accept those private clients.

Backing up a step:: Before you can invite them, you have to talk to them. You have to have some sort of interview process in place. Maybe you are offering a free coaching session, strategy session, or clarity session, or you do a straight up interview. You have to schedule those free sessions and then get them in your calendar.

Backing up a step:: You may need a scheduling tool, and possibly an intake form allowing you to learn more about a prospect before you invite them to actually have access to your calendar. You will need some sort of application in place to kind of screen people and make sure they are a good fit.

Backing up a step:: Before they can become interested in applying, they have to hear about you. How are people going to hear about you? It could be as simple as sending out a few emails over week or two. Maybe you'll also post on social media to let people know you have a few openings in your private client calendar.

Backing up a step:: Before you send the emails you have to write the emails. You've got to make some time to map them out, write them out, load them into your email marketing system, and pre-write and queue up some social media posts.

Backing up a step:: Before you hit send on those emails, you've got to make sure you have your application ready to go. That is the thing people are going to fill out in order for you to read it and make sure they are a perfect fit before you invite them to the interview, before you invite them into your program. The application will go on your Invitation page.

And the first thing you'll need to prepare is the invitation page you'll actually be sending people to. Don't make a sales page instead make an Invitation page. Lay out your offer, who it's perfect for, all the benefits, show some results, and invite the visitor to decide if it's right for them.

A lot of steps, right? But now we have a clear action plan to gain those 5 new clients::

- Write invitation page
- Build invitation page on website
- Create application
- Set up scheduling tool
- Create client agreement
- Write invitation emails + social media posts
- Schedule invitation emails + social media posts
- Host potential client interviews
- Send agreement + invoices

It's a lot of little pieces to get someone enrolled in a one-on-one service, coaching or teaching program. If you don't happen to have something set up already, maybe you need to begin with your mailing list. Maybe you need to get a program to help you schedule people online without having to do a lot of email back and forth. Maybe you need to have some sort of tool to accept applications.

As you start to work on your big idea, I want you to remember that you know what you know, you know what you don't know, but *you don't know what you don't know*. That's where the uncertainty and the fear can come in. It takes so much courage and a lot of faith to launch something new, and put yourself out in the world in a big way.

Just by taking this first step - even if you are just going through the reverse engineering process - you should know up front that there might be some gaps for those things that you just don't know about yet.

Trust that you will figure out those gaps as you move forward. You just have to keep taking that next step in front of you and the next step in front of that and the next step in front of that.

Eventually, any gaps that are missing will come to light and you will be able to go through the entire process to get to your end result. You just have to be willing to learn some of these things as you go.

The final piece that I want you to think about now that you have reverse engineered your 90 day plan is - *As you look at it, could you simplify it even more?*

What I mean by that is, for you to get your big idea out into the world, could you strip it down? Could you bring it to Zen-like simplicity instead of trying to go out the gate with a huge splash, a huge launch, especially if you've never done something of that scale before?

Maybe it is something that you can do a beta test with, with really simple systems and tools, before you go off and invest a lot of time, energy and money when you don't really know how it is going to be received by your community.

For example, maybe instead of trying to put together a huge 21-day video challenge like I created for the <u>Fired Up and Focused Challenge</u>, you could focus on something a little bit more streamlined. Maybe your challenge is delivered by an email only and with just a Facebook group. That's all you need just to test the idea, get your feet wet and see how it works for you. It's all about allowing yourself to be exactly where you are.

Just Start

If you start looking at everyone else around you, you begin to compare yourself to someone who is several steps, or even several years ahead of you. When you do that, you're comparing your beginning to someone else's middle. This can become very self-defeating really, really, quickly. It can set you up for a lot of frustration and overwhelm.

I've seen it over and over again, especially as people are trying to create those more leveraged, passive types of offerings like online training programs or online coaching programs where there are a lot of moving parts that, honestly, you don't know about until you've gone through the process for yourself.

It is so important for you to just go through the process the first time, baby step by baby step, learning as you go and not putting so much pressure on yourself to be way ahead of where you actually are. It will be so much easier if you just accept this key step and make it simple for yourself. *Let it be easy.*

Get Support

There might be some gaps in doing any sort of new project. Things that you don't know how to do, technology that you don't know how to use or simple fixes that you don't know about yet and someone else could do these super-fast.

I can't even tell you how many times, when I first launched the first ever online training program I created, I literally crashed my website five or six times trying to get the stupid PayPal buttons to work correctly.

I was trying to do it all on my own, on a site that was completely custom coded. It wasn't as easy as websites are now. I didn't know what the heck I was doing. It was such a mess. I could have called the designer who put it all together and in a couple of minutes she would have had them up there looking great, but I was being so stubborn convincing myself that it didn't make sense for me to hire her just to put a button on my page. I could do it myself.

It really makes sense to get support when you need it. Especially before you start crashing your website or tearing your hair out because you are not sure how to use the technology that will help you get this thing out into the world.

It might mean that you need to go out there and get a little bit of training. It might mean that you need to find a mentor, a coach, or a mastermind partner who can help you figure out what the entire process is going to look like. It might mean that you need to hire a virtual assistant or a specialist.

It's crucial that you really think about getting support because it will make life and business so much easier for you.

Day 16:: Fired Up & Focused Challenge!

Now that I have gotten off my support soapbox, we're going to get into inspired action.

1. Choose your next big idea. What are you committing to for the next 90 days?

2. Reverse engineer the action steps. From the endpoint all the way to the first step that is sitting right in front of you. Remember, if you don't know all the action steps, it's okay. You will figure it out as you go along and you can always fill in those gaps as you get additional training, additional support or mentorship.

3. Can you simplify it at all? If you can, it will be so much easier for you and your clients. Then the next time you can upgrade and take it to another level.

4. Fill in the gaps. Do you need support? Do you need training? Do you need coaching?

5. Plug it in. This is where you can pull out your calendar, open up your project management program and make sure that you are mapping out each individual baby step, each task, and giving yourself some deadlines to get all of these steps done.

Day 17:: Why Your Marketing Isn't Working

You've poured your heart and soul into creating this amazing THING {program, service, product}. You KNOW it will CHANGE LIVES!

Now you have a new challenge – how to influence someone to buy your thing... and become a client. *Without feeling like a sleeze-ball, pushy, scammy tele-marketer/used carsalesman.*

It turns out, for over 60 years scientists have been researching how and why we decide.

Are we the logical, rational beings we think we are?

Or are there social triggers, cues, that lead us to make certain decisions?

According to Robert Cialdini's book *Influence*, as the sheer volume of information increases exponentially we rely more than ever on 6 universal rules of thumb when it comes to decision making. If you want to cut through the clutter and help people to take action, understanding these 6 shortcuts and integrating them mindfully and ethically into your marketing and communications can dramatically help you to attract more clients.

Here's a few ideas for how you can quickly apply these principles of influence into your mindful marketing plan::

1. Reciprocity.

This is all about giving a no-strings-attached gift. When you give someone something, it builds a social currency. Over time, after you've deposited social currency in the form of great blog posts, newsletters, webinars {or however you're adding value to your community}, when it's time to offer something to your peeps - they already know, like, and trust you.

How can you implement this?

A simple "thank you" note after someone drops in for a class. A bonus training video after someone signs up for your email list. A surprise bonus inside your program.

Reciprocity also goes a long way in developing relationships with people you admire. Giving a shout-out to someone on social media could quickly turn into a get to know you call. Supporting someone for the launch of their program could easily turn into them supporting you during yours. Interviewing them for your community leads to requests to be interviewed for theirs.

2. Scarcity.

If there is less of something, it's more appealing {any teenager being told they can't do or have something can attest to this}. This can be easy to exploit… so be honest and in integrity about the use of scarcity.

How can you implement this?

If there is a real limit to the number of people you can work with – tell them!

For example, I only accept 5 people at a time for my 1x1 Mentorship program. It's not false scarcity; I honestly only have the time and energy available to work with a handful of private clients at this level while still offering other programs, working on other projects, and living a beautifully full life.

Urgency {which is basically scarcity of time to take action} is another proven way to use this principle of influence to get people to take action. This is as simple as letting people know there is an expiration date for your offer. Generally, if there is no reason for people to ACT NOW, they won't!

After launching my program Conscious Business Design over a dozen times, I've realized that as many as 60% of signups come in the last 48 hours before the deadline! This is true across the board - over and over again, my clients experience the same in their launches. Sending that final reminder email is essential to reminding people the deadline is approaching!

Again – I think it's crucial to use scarcity and urgency extremely mindfully. You can quickly cross the line into scammy when there are "*only 100 copies of this e-book!!!!!*" or say "*only 10 spots left*" in a completely virtual on-demand home-study program.

3. Authority.

People follow the lead of knowledgeable experts. This is why we all want to know Oprah's favorite things — because obviously Oprah is FABULOUS so her favorite things must be amazing! We don't even have to think about it.

How can you implement this?

This is why I love teaching mindful marketing – it's all about educating and providing value up front. If someone is searching online for a yoga therapist and they come across your blog that has well-written articles on the exact topics they are looking for – BOOM! You are perceived as an expert!

You can also borrow someone else's authority by aligning yourself with them. Oprah is the perfect example of this – she did not start as an expert at personal development, she was the person who interviewed all the experts. Over time, she started sharing her own experiences and insights. Now she's the queen of personal development.

4. Consistency.

People like to be consistent with what they've already said or done. If they said YES once, they are likely to say YES again.

How can you implement this?

This principle is fantastic for building your word of mouth buzz and is exactly why something like *Click to Tweet* works so well! If someone has already clicked to read your blog post, chances are they will also say yes to sharing your post via *Click to Tweet*.

One of my favorite hidden places for engagement? Your thank you pages. How many times have you signed up for someone's email list just to be taken to a generic thank you page? Instead, use that page to ask people to follow you on social media or share the freebie you gave away {from principle #1 above} with their friends.

5. Liking.

People want to work with other people who they know, like, and trust. This is the biggest indicator that focusing on your dream clients isn't just a warm and fuzzy - it's in your greatest business interest.

How can you implement this?

Get comfortable with a little more vulnerability. Let your hair down. People need to know a little bit about who you are to decide if you are they type of person they want to work with.

For example, by now you know I'm a mamapreneur with 5 year old twins and a 2 year old toddler in tow. You know I'm an introvert who prefers the quiet of working from home. And you know that I'm a yogi who infuses all area of my life and business with mindfulness.

By being open and transparent about who I am outside of just my professional credentials, people connect on a deeper level. This is especially crucial if they are deciding to work with you based on your website and not actually meeting you in real life. The more people can relate to you, the more likely they are to decide to work with you.

6. Consensus.

People are looking for proof that others are doing it too. Yup – we all want to be assured that someone else has taken the leap!

How can you implement this?

Social proof, baby.

This is why so many of us turn to our friends to ask who they recommend - and trust that over our own research. We trust that our friends only recommend someone they know, like, and trust.

But when you're building a business, those referrals are just one way of getting that stamp of social proof::

You can also show off where you've been featured as an expert - *where have you contributed or been interviewed?*

You can show off testimonials from happy clients on your website and invitation pages - *who got amazing results from working with you?*

Day 17:: Fired Up & Focused Challenge!

Now it's time to get into inspired action! Choose 2 areas that you will integrate into your current mindful marketing plan::

1. Reciprocity
2. Scarcity/Urgency
3. Authority
4. Consistency
5. Liking
6. Social Proof

Day 18:: Stop Marketing
+ Start Resonating

The previous chapter's focus, the science of persuasion, is all about how to move people into taking inspired action. But there's a problem…

Marketing just doesn't work for heart-centered entrepreneurs.

This might surprise you. We know that marketing helps us grow our business. In fact, it's been one of the major task areas that we CEOs need to spend our time and energy on if we want to move forward towards our painted picture.

So, what's the problem here? Why am I suddenly saying that marketing doesn't even work for heart-centered entrepreneurs?

Every day, I see the absolute frustration of solopreneurs who get bogged down in all the tips and tricks and tactics. ALL THE THINGS that we're being told we should do to grow our business.

We are told that we have to be on Pinterest, Twitter, Instagram, Facebook, and blogging every day of the week.

Wait, no, we should only blog once a week.

Forget the blog, start a podcast.

Interview others.

No, we need to get interviewed.

No, we need to speak.

No, we need to be doing this and that and this and that.

It is overwhelming!

The problem with tips, tricks, and tactics? There is nothing cohesive to hold it all together. As a result, we start feeling like we are throwing spaghetti at the wall trying to see what sticks.

And when you're always trying out the next shiny new tip or trick or tactic, nothing gets a chance to actually land and gain some momentum.

Amplifying that? Most people only take a fraction second to decide if they are going to stick around long enough to learn more.

We've already talked about how we are more distracted as a society than ever before. Our attention spans have shrunk and--online especially--if you can't engage with somebody in a fraction of a second, there is nothing between you and the back button.

Why do we hate marketing so much?

It's because it feels like an uphill battle. The odds are not stacked in our favor. We are trying to capture people's attention in the super limited timeframes. At the same time we're told the only way to market our business is to contribute to the same noise that is keeping them from paying attention to us.

We're told that we have to do more. Do more blogging. Do more social media. Do more advertising. Do more, do more, do more.

Market Less. Resonate More.

What if, instead, we were able to stop marketing and start *resonating*? This is a word that heart-centered entrepreneurs love because it's more mindfully focused on making a connection with the people you're here to serve.

There is actually science behind resonance.

Resonance is all about frequency. If you take a resonance plate, pour some sand on it, and turn on a frequency - the pile of sand will begin to take this amazing shape. If you change the frequency, you will start to see the sand shift into ever more gorgeous, intricate patterns. It's not forced or coerced into taking action - it happens naturally.

Resonance is all about connecting on this visceral, intuitive level.

If you can tune yourself to the frequency of your dream clients by speaking their language, meeting them exactly where they are, and providing incredible value, then your message can resonate.

When your message resonates - they want to take the next step.

With resonance, you don't have to be another nameless, faceless corporation or big business. Too many heart-centered entrepreneurs try to appeal to as many people as possible because this is what we see as marketing for the bigger companies out there. The result is that we become beige. There is no face attached, there are no personal stories {which is essential for resonance}.

For you to resonate with your audience, they want you to be more of yourself. They want to hear your stories. They want to know, like, and trust you. That is how you will start to connect more deeply with them.

We started talking about tapping into being more of yourself when we discovered your business sweet spot. By now you should have a basic understanding of your passion, your purpose and the people you are meant to serve.

After walking hundreds of heart-centered entrepreneurs through their Business Sweet Spot, I started to see a pattern emerge that helped to simplify everything. It became clear that certain marketing strategies worked beautifully well for some entrepreneurs with a specific type of Business Sweet Spot and there were other strategies to avoid completely.

Discover Your Entrepreneur Sweet Spot Theme

When I share this concept with my Conscience Business Designers, suddenly light bulbs were going off. They understood why marketing wasn't working for them. Once they were able to stop marketing and start resonating, everything became much easier.

I found that most heart-centered entrepreneurs fall into one of these four themes:: the maker, the maven, the mentor, and the mastermind.

Inside Conscious Business Design, we use a few different assessments to determine which theme best fits you and your business… but as you dive in below, one will likely pop out at you.

The Maker {It's All About Follow-Through}

If you are a maker, you love the act of creating something from nothing. You would consider yourself a creator, a doer; somebody who likes to follow through all of the way from start to finish in a project.

You like to see things take shape. You're probably a master at your craft. Whatever it is you do, you have worked really hard to become the best at it and you've invested a lot of time, energy, and money into learning this art.

Often, you are a 'behind the scenes' type of person. Many Makers are drawn to careers like photography, design, make-up artist, stylist, wedding planners, project managers; things that are a little bit more creative in nature.

Your dream clients want you to create *for them*. You have this amazing skill-set that most people don't have. They come to you when they know they can't do it themselves - they want your talent, your eye, your expertise to bring their dream to life.

How can you resonate? By delivering a stellar customer experience, showcasing your work and asking for referrals {in fact if you're work is AMAZING, those referrals will come without asking because you made your client look incredible}.

As a maker, you can stop marketing and you can start creating.

The Maven {It's All About Ideas}

If you are a maven, you love big ideas and getting them out into the world. You're one of the people who are naturally magnetic, charming and inspiring.

You're probably called a ringleader at some point in your life. You might have been the person who was the captain of a sports team. You were the naturally take charge or the person who could rally the troops and get everybody through a tough situations.

Your dream clients want you to *inspire them*. Your dream clients want you to be the leader - they want to rally for your cause. They want you to blaze the trail and to be the voice of a movement.

How can you resonate? By investing your marketing energy into getting on bigger platforms to build your own via interviews, speaking on stage, and contributing to major sites. Your peeps want to see and hear you!

If you are a maven, then you can stop marketing and start inspiring.

The Mentor {It's All About Relationships}

If you are a mentor, then you love encouraging and empowering people. You're probably naturally very nurturing and people are drawn to you because you are a *people* person.

You probably make friends really easily and people come to you when they need support, advice or help. You're probably a teacher or a coach.

Your dream clients want you to *work with them*. They want you to hold their hand, help them be accountable, but also give them a loving kick in the pants when they are getting stuck and need someone who can keep moving them forward.

How can you resonate? By focusing on connections and relationships. Focus on high touch, community focused strategies. You'll thrive connecting and collaborating with like-hearted entrepreneurs. Those relationships will help put you in front of more of the right people!

If you are a mentor, then you can stop marketing and start connecting.

The Mastermind {It's All About The Plan}

If you are the mastermind then you are the type of person who loves taking big ideas and breaking them down into action steps.

You're the person who can look at the big picture and figure out how everything fits together. You're naturally an organizer, a planner and a problem-solver. You love figuring out the puzzle of how you can make this work and how you can get people from A-Z.

Your dream clients want you to *show them how*. They want you to break out the step-by-step, the recipe that they need to follow in order to get where they need to go. The more you can show people exactly how to do what they want to do, how to reach that big picture or achieve that big idea, the more they will resonate and connect with you.

How can you resonate? Always be teaching. Your peeps look to you as a subject matter expert - they want you to do all the research, then give them the bite size insights and inspired action steps. Of all the themes, you'll do best when you're consistently publishing content across multiple platforms {blogging, video, podcast} to facilitate multi-modal learning - but find ways to do the work ONCE and let it work for you multiple ways {like making a video, then turning that into an audio podcast + transcribe into a blog post}.

If you are a mastermind, you can stop marketing and start teaching.

Day 18:: Fired Up & Focused Challenge!

It's time to get into inspired action.

What do you believe your Entrepreneur Sweet Spot Theme might be?

How can you begin using this in your marketing?

Day 19:: Generosity Is
The Best Business Strategy

It used to be that if you were looking for a yoga teacher, a health coach, a holistic healthcare practitioner, if you were looking for a designer or photographer, you'd be limited to people in your town.

Now, when people are looking for someone like you, they start by going online and doing the research. Come to think of it - I don't buy anything without going online and doing some research!

The internet has changed marketing forever.

Aside from the fact that we have to be online - it's just the reality of doing business in 2015 - one of the biggest challenges for us is actually standing out in an online space where there are literally hundreds of thousands of people doing similar types of work.

Once they land on your website, it only takes a fraction of a second for people to decide if they are going to continue learning about you. The odds are really are not stacked in our favor - only 1% of visitors who land on your site will actually press the button and purchase something from you right away.

What about all the other 99% of people who are landing on your site who didn't buy anything?

Remember - marketing is out and resonance is in.

Resonance is essential to creating mindful marketing strategy that actually works. Resonance is the key to capturing their attention instantly; without that instant connection that instantly engages them, you will never be able to build up the know, like, and trust factor that helps people to take the next step.

When we talked about the secret shortcuts to persuasion by Robert Chialdini, we touched on the concept of consistency.

Consistency states that we naturally want to stick to what we said we want to do. It's all about taking one small action and continuing to take action steps along a path. If we say we agree to one thing, we are more likely to agree to the next step along the line.

Remember - it's essential to use these concepts mindfully and ethically if you don't want to come off as a sleezy salesperson. If you've ever taken any sales training, consistency is exploited when the goal is to have the customer answer yes a lot, so that by the time they actually ask for the sale, they've been shaking their head yes so much that they take the bait automatically, really without thinking. It's a dirty, ugly trick that often leads to buyers remorse and rarely return customers.

We would never, ever, go there. What we are talking about is helping people to make small commitments to the things they want - for the help, solution, or support they're looking for - that ultimately lead them to commit to bigger and greater results for themselves. *We can do this with integrity.*

It's all about helping them to feel empowered, educated, and confident about making a decision to work with you.

The strategy I am going to share with you today is all about instantly connecting, engaging, and then nurturing people through that know, like, and trust process so that you can filter out the people who aren't a good fit for you while allowing your dream clients to feel ready to take that next step.

Invite Them to Take Baby Steps

Let's take a look at what a small step looks like in a few different business models.

Do you run a yoga studio or wellness center?

One popular small step is to offer a first class free. You will see this a lot in yoga studios, Pilates studios, wellness centers, and fitness centers. Their intention is just to get you in the door, knowing that once you step in the door and experience the class, you're more likely to sign up for a longer period of time.

Here is the journey from aspirational yogi to paying yoga student::

Yoga studios know that if they offer that first class free, you are more likely to come in, enjoy the yoga class, and take advantage of a new student package. This is really popular in yoga and other fitness and health centers; to offer some sort of incentive for people to take the next small step, which is usually something like an unlimited month of yoga or X number of sessions for a special price.

Once they are officially a new student and experience the studio even more, they are more likely to up level to a full membership. This is a bigger commitment, usually to the tune of several hundred or even several thousand dollars a year.

Why did that first free class work? For a student to come in for that initial first class, there was actually a commitment on their end. Even though they didn't pay any money for that class, they took the time to clear their calendar, to put on their yoga clothes, to bring their yoga mat, to drive all the way to class, find a parking spot, attend the entire class, and then to go home again. *That's a big chunk of time and energy committed.*

Do you offer software as a service?

Free trials are incredibly popular for software. You can sign up for a $0 or even a $1 free trial. In fact, if you've been looking for software for your business a great example of this is email marketing. MailChimp offers a $0 free trial and AWeber offer a $1 free trial.

Why do they do this? Because they know that once you start investing the time and energy to set up your account, you'll make a decision as to whether you are going to continue using that service.

Let's take a look at the journey to a paying client for software, a service, or an app::

Often you'll start with a thirty-day free trial. Once the thirty days are over, you are upgraded into a monthly recurring membership. Most of these platforms understand though that there is still a commitment from the client for you to get the most out of an email marketing service, then you have to go in there, set it up, put all the forms all over your website, import all your lists, set up all your auto responders. It's a lot of work to see if it is going to be a fit for you. They know that even though you didn't put any money out yet, *you've put a lot to time and energy into seeing if it can be a fit.*

They also know that most people looking at software service solutions are actually ready to make a buying decision. Most people don't sign up for a million free trials for similar services, especially when they have to put their credit card information in to make sure that that next monthly payment goes through.

They know that once you are in, you are ready to make a decision as soon as possible. You are actually going to take the time to set it up so that you know that if it is a yes or no before that monthly period is up.

While a free trial works great for software, it's not always the case for those of us who are looking for a way to introduce our teaching, coaching, or services to potential clients.

Are you a teacher, coach, or service provider?

Often, we are told that we should be doing free coaching sessions as much as possible where the whole goal is to get people on the phone. It's a small commitment of usually 20 or 30 minutes where the whole goal is to turn those free coaching sessions, those free introductory sessions, those free consultations into paying clients.

Let's take a look at that journey from free consult to paying client::

Most people do this in a two step process:: 1) Offer a free coaching session and 2) invite those people into the paid program/service. If you have the right person on the phone who is ready to make a buying decision, this can be a great strategy.

But I personally don't love this strategy for every entrepreneur {myself included} as it can often become a big time waster.

The first challenge is just the huge leap you are asking people to take. Unlike a free yoga class or a free software trial, the leap from a free 20 minute session to enrolling into a program or service that is often hundreds, if not thousands, of dollars for a period of three to six to 12 months is a much bigger ask.

If the right person isn't on the other end of the free session, you'll be stressed when you don't get many new clients.

The biggest reason that you'll have the wrong person? They haven't really had a chance to know, like, and trust you via your existing free content. Building a relationship takes time - and that is not going to happen in just a 20 or 30-minute timeframe. Even if it is the most mind-blowing 20-minute session, you are going to have a really challenging time with someone who doesn't have a lot of experience with you yet. That huge leap is the first challenge.

The second challenge is that most people teaching this strategy are not teaching you what you need to do in order to *get people to those free sessions*. Usually, the entire focus is to just tell everybody to just to offer a free session, but there is not really anything to warm those potential clients up to it. There's nothing to help them feel that you are right for them.

When you have people coming to those free coaching sessions and they are not warmed up, they're cold. Which means, they don't know, like, or trust you.

When they come into those conversations without that know, like and trust factor in place, then it is no longer a coaching session. Then it's a sales conversation. For you to get them to the next step, you're going to have to have an intensive sales conversation that is more focused on "closing the deal" than actually making sure that it's a perfect fit for them.

What is that missing piece that would get the right people on to those coaching sessions with you? People, who are warmed up, they know, like and trust you and are in the correct state of mind. They are ready to make a decision to whether or not they want to take the relationship further and take that next step to work with you.

Irresistible Free Offer

There are a lot of different names for this; I've heard it called an Ethical Bribe, Pink Spoon, a Freebie. But I like Irresistible Free Offer or IFO because to me it is more than just some throw away freebie that you cobble together in an hour and post on your website.

It is a real, genuine offer. It's something of great value that serves the people that you want to be working with. It actually allows them to experience what it could be like to work with you, to get a taste.

Then, when they show up for those first consultations, they know you, they like you and they trust you. They've experienced some sort of success with your work already and at that point, it's not a matter of *do they want to sign up for a program*, it's more a matter of *is this the right next step for them*.

An Irresistible Free Offer is all about giving people that taste, that sample of working with you. It allows people to experience your style and a small win.

This is where many people get mixed up. I think they start creating freebies that aren't exciting, they don't help people get any meaningful results and they don't get people excited.

An Irresistible Free Offer should showcase your best work.

It really does need to be your best work. You don't need to hold back on this. I have a lot of people who are worried that they are giving their best stuff away for free. Why would someone actually sign up to work with them? *You've got to remember that there is always more where this came from.*

Even if you give all of your best information away for free, what they really want is YOU at the end of the day. They want access to you. They want your hands on expertise. They want your support. They want to have you helping them tweak everything to fit their situation.

Your Irresistible Free Offer should be your best work because it's a preview of what it's like to work with you. It's a great way to help potential clients feel confident that this is the level of service and experience you're offering once they become paid clients.

Delivering a high-quality IFO is a huge differentiator in your market. There are lots of people who create throw-away freebies. Not so common? An IFO that makes a huge difference in the lives of your dream clients.

When you have an *incredible* free offer, then people are excited about the next step. They're excited to continue listening to you. They're excited to learn more. It accelerates the entire process that people need to go through in that journey to a paying client.

Once they've gone through that irresistible free offer, they should have a stronger feeling for "*Yes, this is what I am looking for. This is the place I want to be. This is the person I want to work with. I'm ready to roll.*"

Or they'll have a strong no. It will filter out the people who are not a perfect fit. The people who just don't get you and they don't get your style.

This is important because the last thing you want is to have people enrolling into your programs or your services who aren't a great fit. Then you are going to end up with a lot of refunds and a lot of clients you don't enjoy.

Creating Your Irresistible Free Offer

What could your Irresistible Free Offer look like? There are a lot of options available to you and it really depends on your Entrepreneur Sweet Spot Theme, what kind of things you offer and what your natural Mindful Marketing style is.

Quizzes. Who doesn't love to take a quiz? They can be addictive and share-worth. The challenge there is making sure that it actually is valuable enough to get people to take the next step, which could be getting on the phone with you or learning about an offer that you have.

eBook. These don't have to be hundreds of pages - it could be a 15-20 page guide. The challenge here with eBooks is that they are harder for people to get through. You have to remember that the goal of an Irresistible Free Offer isn't just to grab an email address so that somebody can download an eBook that sits on their computer and they never look at it. The goal is to actually give them something valuable that gives them a taste of what it is like to work with you.

Checklists + Cheat Sheets. You are just giving them what they are specifically asking for. Shortening the learning curve for them and giving your best recommendations for things that you recommend using. These are really, really easy to create and put together. You have to be careful here because while they're helpful, they make it easier for people and they can be an easy thing to offer, they aren't necessarily super high value.

Webinars + Teleseminars. These are great options especially if you're wanting to give people a taste of what it's like to work with you in a paid coaching program or online course. They are a little more complicated and require a bit of practice, but highly valuable.

Free Course. This is hands down my personal favorite {see the Fired Up and Focused Challenge} but admittedly, this is a more advanced strategy. It's much more time intensive to create but if you're offering high-end programs or services, this is worth the time and energy to create.

These are some of my favorite ways, personally, to create your Irresistible Free Offer because I find that they're very congruent with most of the healing, helping, teaching and coaching types of entrepreneurs that I work with.

Day 19 Fired Up and Focused Challenge!

It's time to get into inspired action.

What is that commitment journey for your peeps? Map out the steps they need to take from first hearing about you to being ready to sign up and work with you.

What is an Irresistible Free Offer that you think will help accelerate that know, like and trust factor for potential new clients? Focus on IFOs that help warm them up to you, your style, and help them feel like you're exactly who they are looking for.

Day 20:: Why You've Gotta Show {Not Tell}

Imagine that you are your dream client.

You've actually slipped into her shoes and let's say you are looking for a yoga teacher or health coach or doula or a website designer or whatever it is that you actually do. You are actually searching for that professional who can help you solve a problem.

You don't happen to have a friend or a family member to give you a referral. There's no one in your circle that you can think of who knows a professional like this that you can work with, but you know you need someone. You hop online and you start Googling.

The truth is, if someone is searching for you, they are not just finding you. They are actually finding you plus several other people who do similar types of work.

It's really important that you figure out how to stand out from the crowd so that you're the one getting the phone calls, emails, and new clients.

Your Dream Clients Are Looking for Authority + Consensus

Authority basically means that people will follow a credible expert. The hard part? You can't just run around saying *"Hey, I'm an expert. Follow me; I know what I am taking about."* No one really likes that and people aren't inclined to believe you. They feel like you are tooting your own horn. They want to hear it from a third party, an outside source. That actually lends more credibility to you.

Which leads us to consensus. Consensus shows that others have worked with you and gotten some results. Someone else has actually opened their wallet to sign up and take that next big step. This is important because people are hesitant to take that step of reaching out and connecting and working with you if there's no proof that what you do is actually worth it and you can deliver on your promise.

You need to show that you've taken someone else through a process, through a system, through a program or done something with them and given them what they wanted..

When you bring together authority and consensus, then you are having a way to show that you are both credible and have gotten people results.

The Power of Testimonials

Let's take a look deeper at this because the truth is, not all testimonials are created equal. Many testimonials that you'll hear are very vague. Even if someone loves working with you, they can give you a testimonial that won't help you to turn the casual reader into someone who is ready to take that next step and learn about working with you.

Here is an example of a vague testimonial::

"Racheal's just awesome! That's all I have to say. There is a special place in heaven just for you. I loved working with you."

It sounds nice and it strokes my ego a little bit, but at the end of the day they are fluffy. There is not real substance. There is nothing in there that helps somebody get the feeling that you can genuinely help them. That is because we're missing out on some key elements.

Let's look at some amazing testimonials and then break them down so that you can learn how to ask for testimonials that will build your business and encourage people to take that next step in the right way.

This is from one of my own clients, Francesca Cervero who is a private yoga teacher and a teacher trainer. Here is what she says,

"When I started I was over worked, over scheduled and exhausted. I felt trapped in the business I had created with no clear direction of how things could shift so I didn't have to work 80 plus hour weeks. I loved my business and my clients, but I couldn't enjoy any of it because I was so depleted myself.

My life and business have changed completely since working with Racheal. I'm happier, calmer. I'm making more money and moving my business in an exciting new direction. Racheal gave me permission and support to grow my business in the direction that I was most excited about, teaching other teachers. I had been worried that moving in that direction wasn't a smart business choice, but Racheal showed me not only was it a good idea, it was the only way I could grow my business successfully and enjoy myself as I did.

She had helped me break down all my goals in organized, achievable, steps and has made the whole process fun and easy. I have a long list of things I am excited to do and always get them done. As a result, my business has completely transformed within months."

Amazing testimonial, right? We will break down why this works.

1:: There is a clear BEFORE picture.

She tells you she was overworked, over scheduled and exhausted. She felt trapped. She loved her business, but felt depleted. *These are feeling words.* Remember people don't make major decisions based on the logical side. We have to connect with them, with how they are actually feeling. This is a state that many of my clients are feeling before they reach out to work with me inside of Conscious Business Design. It makes it a great testimonial because people can relate to this.

2:: There is a clear AFTER picture.

"I am happier, calmer, making more money and moving my business in as exciting new direction." This is the after picture that most of my dream clients want to experience! Less stress. More success.

3:: It previews the process.

She shares what that experience was like by saying, *"She helped me break down all my goals into organized achievable steps and has made the whole process fun and easy."* This really helps people to see what the experience is like working with me. They get a feeling, in a preview clients words, about what exactly she found most valuable working with me.

Let's take a look at another one and then we will deconstruct it a little bit. Meet Casey Berglund, she is an amazing nutritionist and health coach. Here is what she says,

"Before Conscious Business Design, I was a one man show who said yes to anything and everything I could, even at the expense of my own self-care. Because of my fear of getting too niched I took on clients who weren't a perfect fit for what I had to offer. I did not have the business knowledge or tools I needed to simplify my schedule, build systems or get support. I felt scattered, overwhelmed and often drained.

Through Conscious Business Design, I discovered where I best serve in this world and have committed myself to that purpose. I had a total breakdown part way through where I questioned everything about my business and my life. Racheal was there for me. She reminded me that this is part of the process and helped me get back on track. I feel like I have a clear path ahead and the support I need for the journey.

Here is to celebrating a full private client docket. A team I can count on and the space in my calendar for me time, friend time and family time. I have Racheal and Conscious Business Design to thank."

This is an amazing testimonial. Here is why it is so powerful.

1. There is a clear BEFORE picture.

She says, "*I was a one man show who was saying yes to everything at the expense of my own self-care.*" She says, "*I had fear of going too niched.*" She says, "*I didn't have business knowledge, tools to simplify my schedule, build systems or get support.*"

There is a lot in this before picture. But again, this is where many people are when they are learning about a program like Conscious Business Design. It's completely relatable - potential clients will definitely feel like this is describing exactly where they are when they are reading this testimonial.

2. There is a clear AFTER picture.

She shares the after picture - "*Celebrating a full private client docket, a team she can count on and space for me time, friend time and family time.*" I love it! You instantly feel the relief and the power that she now has for herself; feeling like she's in control of her business and her life.

3. It previews the process.

I also love this more personal piece where she goes in and shares when she had breakdown and she was questioning everything. This is common for people when they are going through a program like Conscious Business Design. This is one of the worries that a lot of people might have looking at a high level program - will it guide them through the uncertainty? Will it help when you get stuck?

She actually gives reassurance by telling people that I was there for her. When you have a testimonial that actually acknowledges that there might have been challenges going through this process, but that you were able to help them get to the other side, it's really giving a look into what the experience will be like for them.

Let's look at one final testimonial and then we're going to talk about the questions that you need to give people in order to get testimonials that are this powerful.

The final one is from Kathy Stowell, an amazing Mama Bliss coach who recently started coaching other coaches::

"My business was in the throes of a year's long spaghetti throwing to see what sticks phase. There were some successful throws, but this go to tactic was making quite the mess wasting a lot of money and leaking my confidence. Probably the biggest struggle in finding success was knowing exactly what to focus on. Me being the hyper creative, I always feel I have a million ideas percolating inside me at all times and the mama in me wants to birth them all.

The biggest difference was being more mindful about my marketing. I love the process outlined in Conscious Business Design. The way Racheal guided us through it helped click it all together for me; knowing which offerings, marketing strategies and ideal peeps to meditate on during my precious working hours.

Racheal, in Conscious Business Design, offered me a path to follow by a woman who gets the heart-centered nature of the online work I am involved in. My income has double from last year thanks to the clarity and insight I found in Conscious Business Design."

Another great testimonial and you will see the same structure.

1. There is a clear BEFORE picture.

She shares her before picture- *this year long spaghetti throwing to see what sticks phase*. It was creating a mess. She was not confident. This is so completely relatable to many entrepreneurs who are in that stage of business.

2. There is a clear AFTER picture.

Her income doubled over last year! That's a concrete result that is something many of my dream clients desire. It's something they have likely written down on their own vision boards and in numerous goal setting sessions.

3. It previews the process.

You also get a peek into the program itself. "*The way Racheal guided us through it helped it all click together.*" This is a major issue many of my dream students have attempting to figure everything out themselves through books or self-study programs… they can't seem to see how all the elements fit together into a manageable system.

Day 20:: Fired Up & Focused Challenge!

How do we start getting you testimonials like this? What's actually in the great testimonials that you want to make sure you are gathering from your favorite clients? We've seen the three main elements in great testimonials - now let's help you get more of them for your own biz!

It all starts with having questions. The reason you shouldn't just say, "*Hey, I'd love to get a testimonial from you*," is people freeze up. They don't know what to write. We are not all naturally geared towards singing the praises of other people in the way that resonates for us trying to market and grow our businesses.

By giving people prewritten questions, you are actually making it easier for them to let you know and to let future clients know what they really experience. This is how you avoid those vague testimonials.

Here's some example questions - feel free to mix and match to begin collecting amazing testimonials from your clients!

1. Establish a BEFORE picture.

What was the biggest challenge you faced before working with me?

What was the worst part about that?

What was that holding you back from in your life/health/business?

2. Establish the AFTER picture.

What changes or results have you seen after working with me?

What did you celebrate after wrapping our work together?

What has made the biggest impact in your life/health/business?

3. It should PREVIEW the experience.

What is the most important thing people should know about working with me?

What was your favorite part about working with me?

What surprised you the most about working with me?

Today's Challenge - Ask three to five former clients for testimonials!

Day 21:: Celebrate Your Sweet Success!

It's time to celebrate!

It's so exciting and bittersweet that you've wrapped up 21 Days of Fired Up & Focused. I know you've experienced a TON of growth, not only in your productivity and biz skills, but in flexing those CEO muscles!

Today is your day to review, reflect, and remind yourself of how far you've come in just a few short weeks. Now that you've gone through this process, are you more aware of how you spend your days in your business? Have you implemented the systems to streamline and simplify your business? Are you rockin' out your pomodoros?

Progress Not Perfection!

After running The Fired Up & Focused Challenge live, I noticed that many of our alumni Challengers would come back again and again. Some only completed a few days the first time through, focusing on implementing the crucial CEO time management lessons. Others would repeat the Challenge as a way to jumpstart their next 90-day plan.

This book is here for you to refer to again and again as you begin implementing these success practices into your daily routines. Go back and review! I promise you'll continue to get new insights and inspiration that you may have missed the first time through.

Insight + Inspired Action = Momentum

If you haven't popped over to grab your book bonuses, including the Fired Up & Focused Workbook and CEO Planner, make sure you do that today {http://www.firedupandfocused.com/book}!

It's so easy to edu-tain yourself, skimming through a book like this, nodding your head thinking *"Oh that's a good idea".* Good ideas don't build businesses! Only taking consistent inspired action will get you where you want to go.

Just because we're at Day 21, doesn't mean that growth stops. Consider today the launching pad. As you float down from your Fired Up & Focused high, let's do a quick review of the top lessons from Fired Up & Focused::

From Solopreneur to CEO

Even if you're a team of one - you are the BOSS. If you find yourself in the day-to-day busy work of your business every single day of the week, then it means you're dramatically limiting the impact {and yes - the income} you can make with your business.

In the first few days of Fired Up and Focused, we talked about those 20% tasks that make 80% of the impact in your business. If you're not dedicating time each and every week to work on the big picture of your business, you'll find yourself creating a ceiling to your success!

Start where you are - even if all you have is 30 minutes a day or 2 1/2 hours a week to do the big picture work in your business, you'll start to see a big shift within just a few short month and reach your goals faster than you thought possible.

Systematize, Streamline, Simplify

The #1 reason for stressed out, overwhelmed entrepreneurs? Busy work. Un-ending piles of administrative, operations, and customer service tasks.

By taking the time to make a system once, you'll find that you can more quickly get these tasks off your plate and as you grow, hand them off to an amazing assistant.

Keep Your Eyes on Your Own Paper

It's so incredibly hard to not get distracted by all the things vying for your attention. There's a new tip or trick or tactic every single day. There are people sharing their inspirational success stories, promising to teach you exactly how they did it.

Remember, your role as the CEO is to stay focused on your definition of success. When you have a clear vision for the future, it's so much easier to ignore all the distractions.

Your One Year Painted Picture is there to be your north star. Break it down into 90 Day Action Plans {see your bonus workbook}. Get the support and skills you need to continue taking action, but make sure it all aligns with your bigger vision.

Fail to Plan = Plan to Fail

A little bit of planning goes a long way in ensuring you are making consistent forward momentum towards your goals!

Now that you have a clearly prioritized To Do List as well as your Must Do Tomorrow List, you should know exactly what you need to work on when you sit down to work every single day.

Every week, make a CEO date with your business to check your weekly plans against your bigger 90 Day and 1 Year Painted Picture.

Remember - we easily over estimate what we can get done in a day or week, but underestimate what we can accomplish in a year of consistent inspired action!

Stop Marketing. Start Resonating.

If there is one core task that is like rocket-fuel to your business - it's marketing. But shameless self-promotion? ICK.

When you understand the power of resonance, you can stop marketing and instead play to your most fascinating strengths that magnetically attract your dream clients. We discussed the Entrepreneur Sweet Spot Themes::

Maker. You're a natural implementer who loves to create something from nothing. Your dream clients want you to do FOR them. When your creations make your dream clients look amazing {and you WOW with your customer experience}, watch out for a flood of referrals.

Maven. You're naturally magnetic and charismatic, with presence that commands an entire room. Your dream clients want you to INSPIRE them. Your big ideas are meant for a big platform, where you'll build a movement with your message.

Mentor. You're naturally warm, welcoming, and nurturing. Your dream clients want you to be there right alongside them, holding their hand, helping them navigate each step of the way. Your business craves connection; high touch and in person strategies will always make the biggest impact.

Mastermind. You're a fixer. A planner. A problem-solver. Your dream clients come to you when they want to know HOW to do something. When you can create processes and frameworks, you can reach and teach your dream clients across almost every media format available.

Live In Your Business Sweet Spot

Too often, entrepreneurs find themselves struggling to squeeze their business into someone else's plan. When your business isn't 100% tailored to fit you - it's way harder than it needs to be!

You have all the pieces of the puzzle to find the intersection between your passion, your purpose, and the people you're meant to serve. When you truly embrace your Business Sweet Spot, you'll find more freedom, ease, and abundance.

Hugs and Highfives!

There's no challenge today - just a big virtual hug and highfive! You've got everything you need to get {and stay} Fired Up & Focused in your business.

Exclusive Fired Up & Focused Book Bonuses!

Your copy of Fired Up & Focused includes access to exclusive book bonuses. Claim your bonuses at http://www.firedupandfocused.com/book

The Fired Up & Focused Challenge

This book is based on the 21 Day Fired Up & Focused Challenge - a full video course delivered straight to your inbox! When you join the Challenge, you'll also get access to our incredible private community of like-hearted entrepreneurs.

The Fired Up & Focused Workbook

Ready to accelerate your Fired Up & Focused success? We've created a beautiful workbook to help you implement everything from this book, including all the exercises as well as some bonus worksheets to help you map out your 90 Day Plan!

CEO Planner

As you begin implementing the Fired Up & Focused strategies into your work routine, the CEO Planner will help you maintain your new work habits!

Deep Gratitude

So much love and gratitude for all the amazing people who have supported me throughout this crazy journey of entrepreneurship, but most especially to my husband, Jameson for being a source of unconditional love and encouragement.

Thank you to my entire team:: Lane Clark-Bonk, Suzi Istvan, Amber Kinney, Maggie Patterson, and Katie Truman. I'm so grateful to have each of you supporting me and sharing your greatest talents to help get this message out into the world.

And to all the amazing Challengers, past, present, and future. You are the reason I do the work that I do!

About Racheal Cook

Racheal Cook, MBA is a green smoothie enthusiast, restorative yoga advocate, and award winning business strategist who believes entrepreneurs can grow their dream business while living their dream life, right now.

After experiencing debilitating anxiety and burnout in her former life in the traditional corporate world, Racheal walked away from a lucrative consulting career and onto a yoga mat. Months later, she married her passion for yoga and business acumen by launching The Yogipreneur, a boutique consultancy teaching the yoga of business and mindful marketing.

Since launching TheYogipreneur.com in 2008 then RachealCook.com in 2014, she's built two multiple six-figure business inspiring over 10,000 entrepreneurs around the world to create profitable, sustainable businesses they can be proud of. Her work has been featured on Female Entrepreneur Association, US Chamber of Commerce, Lady Business Radio, Smart Passive Income, The Rise To The Top, and Entrepreneur on Fire.

When she's not sharing her latest insights on business and lifestyle design, you can find Racheal practicing yoga with her three kidlets, reading everything she can get her hands on, and experimenting with new green smoothie recipes {spinach, avocado, and pineapple is her fav!}.

Visit Racheal's home on the web::
RachealCook.com

Connect with Racheal on social media::

Facebook
Twitter
Instagram
Pinterest

Printed in Great Britain
by Amazon.co.uk, Ltd.,
Marston Gate.